ANALYSIS OF GREAT PHILOSOPHERS

Analysis of Great Philosophers

Rajyashri Agrawal

ANMOL PUBLICATIONS PVT. LTD.
NEW DELHI - 110 002 (INDIA)

ANMOL PUBLICATIONS PVT. LTD.
4374/4B, Ansari Road, Daryaganj
New Delhi - 110 002
Ph.: 23261597, 23278000
Visit us at: www.anmolpublications.com

Analysis of Great Philosophers

First Published, 2006

ISBN 81-261-2568-3

PRINTED IN INDIA

Published by J.L. Kumar for Anmol Publications Pvt. Ltd., New Delhi - 110 002 and Printed at Arora Offset Press, Delhi.

Contents

Preface

I realized the importance of analysis during my early college days, not only in the field of Philosophy but in every sphere.

While in post graduation my interest and curiosity for the immense importance of analysis saw an increase. It is this urge that led to a research on a topic related with Analysis - special reference to logical empiricism of A.J. Ayer.

Many philosophers in the 20th century were classified as analysts but in fact analysis has been in existence and has played a very important role from the very beginning. This book "Analysis of Great Philosophers" is a result of my approach towards understanding the subject.

I would like to express my deep sense of gratitude to all my teachers and colleagues who have guided me to be what I am today. I am refaining from mentioning names as it will be unjust if I miss out on some.

I would also like to thank my family for being supportive to this effort of mine.

I hope my readers would like this work — the way they have supported me in my previous books and publications.

—Author

1
Introduction

Throughout in the history of Western philosophical tradition, empiricism has always been an important trend and played an important role in providing solutions to different philosophical problems. Although the main interest of the empiricists has always been epistemological, but their analysis and formulations of philosophical problems had a remarkable bearing on metaphysical problems. In fact, quite a substantial contribution to the development of Western philosophy is made by a conflict of rationalists and empiricists. In order to meet the challenges from each other, both the retionalists and empiricists had to sharpen their logical weapons so that they could justify their philosophical positions. Empiricism, both as a theory as well as philosophical trend, is as old as philosophy itself. The empiricists attach supreme value to the truth of sense-experience and then try to justify its supremacy with their intellectual might. In this process they had to solve all those philosophical problems which were presented to them by the rationalistic a priorism.

Although empiricism in its seed form is found in the Greek period of Western philosophy, but it is only in the modern period that we find a mature expression of empiricism in the writings of such eminent philosophers as Bacon, Hobbes, Locke, Berkeley and Hume etc. The philosophy of David Hume is the most powerful expression of the classical emiricism in the eighteen century. For quite a long time it was taken for granted that the solutions of philosophical problems provided by David

Hume along the line of empiricism were final. No less a philosopher than Immanuel Kant admitted that Hume woke him from his dogmatic slumber and he used all his genius to undo the arguments of Hume which, in the opinion of most of the philosophers, proved disastrous to the foundations of rationalism.

After Kant, empiricism seems to have become weak as a philosophical trend and it is the philosophy of Hegel, which as a legacy as well as development of the Kantian position, that remained influential in the West for quite a long time. Most of the subsequent philosophical trends appeared as reactions to Hegelianism. Important among these reactions are Pragmatism, Realism, Critical Realism, Dialectial Materialism, Phenomenology, Existentialism and Logical Empiricism. Logical empiricism is the latest expression of the tradition of empiricism in western philosophy.

In the twentieth century empiricism emerges as a powerful movement of thought equipped with the techniques of modern mathematics, latest researches in the field of logical analysis and modern science. In 1931 Blumberg and Herbert Feigl used the term "logical positivism" for a set of philosophical ideas put forth by the Vienna Circle. Alternatively it is also called "scientific empiricism," "consistent empiricism," "logical empiricism," and "logical neo-positivism." The term logical empiricism is loosely used to include the analytical or ordinary language philosophies recently developed at Cambridge and Oxford.

The growth of logical empiricism as a systematic philosophical movement is traced back to a group of philosophers at Vienna who gave themselves the name of Vienna Circle. This was a group of philosophers, scientists, logicians and mathematicians. The Vienna Circle came into existence in 1920's under the leadership of Professor Mortis Schlick. Other leading members of the movement were Rudolf Carnap, Otto Neurath, Herbert Feigl, Friedrich Waismann, Edger Zilsel, Victor Kraft, Phillipp Frank, Karl Menger, Kurt

Godel and Hans Hahn. It was more of a club than an organised philosophical movement. In 1929, the members of the circle formally registered themselves as a philosophical party. After that they met regularly and discussed the problems of philosophy. The Vienna Circle organised its first international conference in 1929 at Prague and brought out a manifesto entitled "Wissenschaftliche Wellauffassung, Der Wiener Kreis"—The Vienna Circle; its scientific outlook. This publication presented an outline of the philosophical position of the movement.

Alfred Jules Ayer is a powerful exponent of logical empiricism in England. He attended the meetings of the Vienna Circle since 1933. The movement which was initiated by Schlick finds its mature expression in its moderate form in the writings of A.J. Ayer. He has attempted to establish the philosophical position of logical empiricism in his works - Language, Truth and Logic. The Foundations of Empirical knowledge, Philosophical Essays, The Problem of Knowledge, The Concept of a Person, The Origins of Pragmatism, Metaphysics and Common Sense, Russell and Moore: the Analytical Heritage, Probability and Evidence, Russell, and The Central Questions of Philosophy. Through his writings Ayer represents the central position of the philosophy of logical empiricism and has helped in making it a popular movement in the present century.

This movement includes the anti-transcendental and empirical views of Hume, Mill, Mach and James, and the analytical methods of scientific thinkers like Helm Holts, Poincare and Einstein, of mathematical philosophers and symbolic logicians like Frege, Russell and Whitehead, of the contemporary realists like Moore and the American neorealists. It was also deeply influenced by the writings of Wittgenstein. Ludwig Wittgenstein was never officially a member of Vienna Circle, but due to his close personal relations with Schlick and Waismann, the group was very much influenced by his ideas.

Logical positivism is a combination of empiricism and logical analysis. And it is for this reason that this movement is called 'Logical Empiricism'. The credit for this combination goes to Wittgenstein. He felt that there must be a relationship between language and facts. This aim in view, he wrote Tractatus-Logico-Philosophicus which first appeared in 1921. This work left a deep impact on the philosophical thinking of contemporary period.

Wittgenstein's work is regarded as an attempt to construct the rules of an exact language for the criticism of metaphysics, because it affirms that "Most of the propositions and questions arise from our failure to understand the logic of our language."[1] According to him "All philosophy is a critique of language."[2] He says, "Philosophy is a battle against the bewitchment of our intelligence by means of language."[3]

Ayer accepts that the function of philosophy is not to put forward a special set of "philosophical" propositions but to make other propositions clear."[4] This was also the view of G.E. Moore. He did use analysis in his philosophical thinking not for the discovery of some 'new facts' about the universe but only to clarify conceptual confusions. Logical empiricists themselves accept the contribution of Moore in this context. Ayer maintains that philosophy as a linguistic analysis "owes something to the examples of G.E. Moore."[5] But for Moore, analysis was only one of the functions of philosophy. According to him, philosophy is not concerned merely with linguistic expressions but also with the concepts, or propositions or facts for which they stand. In Moore's view, a philosopher who had no mastery of language would be as helpless as a mathematician who could not handle numerals: but just as the mathematician was not concerned with numerals as such but rather with the numbers which they represented, so the philosopher's command of language was merely a necessary means to the investigation of the objective properties of concepts.[6] According to logical empiricists, "The question with which philosophers have really been concerned when they have tried to develop 'Theories of Truth' are questions of testability and meaning."[7]

Every philosophical movement has its two sides—constructive and destructive. In order to construct his own philosophy a philosopher refutes the views of his opponents. Logical empiricism has also two sides. Logical empiricists attempt to destroy the metaphysical doctrines of their predecessors and contemporary thinkers, and then they try to construct their own views with the help of the method of logical analysis of language. The two aims of logical empiricism are to provide a secure foundation for the sciences and to demonstrate the meaninglessness of all metaphysics.

In the second chapter of the present work entitled "The Nature of Philosophical Analysis," the discussion begins with the general nature of philosophical analysis. In the twentieth century logical empiricists claim that the only method of philosophy is linguistic analysis. According to them every branch of knowledge has its own method. Philosophy differs from other arts and sciences by its method. Science adopts the method of observation and scientific theories are tested by observation. For the logical empiricists the method of philosophy is the method of analysis and philosophical theories are tested by analysis. The statements of philosophy do not consist in formal demonstration as of science. A philosopher does not describe a fact. But he analyses 'what do we mean by fact. But in doing so he does not compile as dictionary. A philosopher does not intend to give the dictionary meaning of any word but he seeks to give an analysis of its meaning.

Analysis has always played an important role in the development of philosophical thought. Socrates was concerned with such questions as, 'What is Justice? 'What is knowledge?' and so on. Since the very beginning of philosophy all great philosophers made use of analysis, though their analyses are of different types. Sometimes analysis is used in purely formal way, as it is said that the function of philosophy is merely to provide formal definitions of particular concepts. Others, though they do accept formal analysis, think that definition alone is not sufficient, but a particular concept needs its justification too. Analysis is also used in its informal sense as found in the analysis of ordinary language, where a philosopher is concerned with language which is spoken by ordinary people.

Sometimes analysis is associated with the theory of knowledge through which a philosopher intends to give a satisfactory definition of knowledge, to determine what types of propositions can be known to be true and to explain how they can be known to be true. But in the recent times analysis is much emphasized by the logical empiricists. According to them the only function of philosophy is analysis. And it is for this reason that twentieth century is characterised as an "age of analysis" in philosophy.

The more recent tendency of some philosophers turn philosophy into linguistic analysis. The originators of the movement of analysis were Russell and Moore. It was Moore who for the first time put the meaning of metaphysical propositions to serious criticisms. Before Moore, metaphysics was rejected on the grounds that it transcends the limits of human knowledge or it contradicts our human knowledge, but no one was concerned with its meaning. He used the method of analysis to clarify conceptual confusions. In Russell's philosophy too, analysis was the fundamental event which came in the form of the theory of description. He assumed that 'the meaning of a name is to be identified with the object which the name denotes.' After that in 1922, it was claimed by Wittgenstein that 'philosophy is not a doctrine but an activity.' And then, under the influence of Wittgenstein, logical empiricists made similar claims.

In 1936, Professor Ayer in his Language, Truth and Logic, gave a new description of philosophy in terms of activity of philosophizing and philosophizing is an activity of analysis. In his view the function of a philosopher is "to clarify the propositions of science by exhibiting their logical relationships, and by defining symbols which occur in them."[8] Thus in logical empiricism analysis comes in the form of logical analysis of language. The main purposes of logical analysis are—to eliminate metaphysical propositions and to clarify conceptual confusions. Ayer shows that other types of analysis do not fulfil these aims of philosophy, for they are, in some way, misleading. Logical analysis of language fulfils these aims. Though to some extent analysis has influenced contemporary philosophical thought, and Gilbert Ryle and John Wisdom are the examples of this influence, but it has its own shortcomings. The linguistic analysis, too, could not fulfill the function of philosophy, which I have attempted to evaluate at the end of the chapter.

The third chapter of the thesis is 'The Arguments against the Possibility of Metaphysics.' Ayer denies the possibility of philosophy as a speculative discipline. But the rejection of philosophy as a speculative discipline is also nothing new, because such a concept of philosophy was criticised by some philosophers during the Greek period, although their arguments were different. In this chapter, besides Ayer, I have discussed the anti-metaphysical thesis of Kant and Hume.

Such a change in attitude from metaphysical to anti-metaphysical has been gradual and development of science played an important role in the change of this attitude. As Herbert Feig writes, "To the empiricist one of the most gratifying trend in the history of science is the gradual liberation of theory from metaphysical bondage. The ideas of absolute space, time and substances, of numbers as real entities, of the cause effect relation as an intrinsic necessity, or vital forces and entelechies, and of the manner of obscure faculties and mythical powers — were either *adhoc* explanation or samples of verbal legerdemain or both."[9] The novelty of logical empiricism is that it emphasises upon analysis of meaning and the logical structure of language. "The systematic pursuit of the problem of meaning by means of a logical analysis of language distinguishes Logical Empiricism from earlier more psychological oriented, types of empiricism...."[10] The empiricism of Hume was psychological whereas the empiricism of Ayer is logical. Ayer does not entirely agree with Hume and he finds many difficulties and mistakes in Hume and tries to remove them in his empiricism.

Ayer's criticism of metaphysics "is primarily an attack upon confusions of meanings and not intended as a wholesale repudiation of what has been presented under the label."[11] He formulates a principle, i.e. a principle of verification to verify a meaning of a proposition, according to which the meaning of a proposition depends upon its verification.

Ayer advocates the verification theory of meaning to bring clarity in thinking and to eliminate metaphysical propositions. He divides all meaningful propositions into analytic and empirical types. Only analytic propositions are certain because they are more tautologies. Empirical propositions are true or false probable hypotheses. And the propositions which are neither analytic nor empirical hypothesis, are meaningless or "Pseudo propositions." Metaphysical propositions are meaningless because they come under the category of "pseudo propositions."

The prime source of metaphysical propositions is, according to Ayer, linguistic confusions. Metaphysicians do not want to write such meaningless non-sensical propositions but they are misled by the superficial grammatical features of language. The argument of "pseudoproposition" does not apply only against the possibility of metaphysical propositions, but also against the possibility of ethical, religious and aesthetic propositions. For ethics, religion aesthetics, all these branches believe in the existence of super natural entities in some manner or the other. Ayer's verification theory of meaning has some defects and I have attempted critical evaluation of the theory at the end of the chapter.

The fourth chapter on 'Perception' deals with the different questions concerning the problem of perception. In this context, the main questions with which a philosopher is concerned are - the nature of physical object and human experience and the relation between them. Though all systems of philosophy dealt with this problem, but in realism and empiricism it occupies a place of great importance. For an idealist physical objects are mind-dependent. They are not real but only appearances. And since he denies the reality of them, there is no question of their nature and experience. On the other hand, a realist holds the independent existence of the physical world. Therefore, he has to face the problems of perception.

The philosophers, who accept the reality of physical world, have formulated their views in different theories such as common-sense theory, casual theory, sense-datum theory, and phenomenalism. To establish his own view Ayer examines other views and shows what are the contributions of them to solve the problem of philosophy, and what are the defects and difficulties. The common sense theory holds that we perceive physical objects directly. Objects are perceived as they really are. But this theory is untenable as it fails to explain dream, illusion, etc. This theory is generally refuted by the argument from illusion. Casual theory denies the common sense view, but it is also defective. This theory is based on the scientific explanation that, most probably, things are not as they seem to be and perception is casually dependent upon other factors too. But by this, science does not prove that even in normal conditions we do not perceive physical objects as they really are. Ayer agrees with this scientific fact that physical object are not directly perceived; what we directly perceive is something else. Sense-datum theorists also accept that physical objects are perceived indirectly. But to some extent, Ayer also differs from them.

Ayer uses the word 'sense datum' in such a way that there can be no doubt that sense-data actually are experienced. The purpose to introduce the term 'sense-data', according to Ayer, is to explain the problems about illusion. Things may appear to have qualities which they do not really have or they may appear to exist when they do not really exist.

In Ayer's view, veridical or delusive perception is admitted only with regard to physical object, not with regard to sensedata. For the propositions which describe presented sensedata are indubitable or incorrigible. These propositions are regarded as "basic proposition." But basic propositions are not indubitable in the same way as a priori propositions are indubitable because they are mere tautologies, they say nothing about the fact, whereas basic propositions are indubitable because it is logically incorrect to doubt the truth of a proposition which describes a present sense-datum. The propositions like 'I perceive —' can be doubted. It can be said that I was having an illusion, but the propositions like 'It seems to me —' cannot be doubted. Thus basic propositions are empirical propositions pertaining to sense data, as I feel, I see, and they are indubitable or certain, because they cannot be doubted. In this context, he also deals with the problem whether sensing is a kind of knowing. And to avoid the confusion he makes use of the words sensation or awareness in connection with sense-data, perception in connection with physical objects, and knowledge in connection with propositions.

Ayer also deals with phenomenalism. Phenomenalism holds that physical objects are logical construction out of sense data. It claims that every empirical statement about a physical object is reducible to a statement or set of statements, which refer exclusively to sense data. But this theory has its own difficulties. When no one perceives an object, as pencil, when there are no sense data that are directly relevant to its existence, the pencil may still exist. Thus phenomenalism is not illuminating. Ayer is a phenomenalist in the sense that he does assert the existence of physical objects as logical construction out of sense-data. But, on the other hand, he also criticises its thesis of reductionism. In Ayer's view, physical objects are logical construction out of sense data in the sense that there is no such object which is or was, under any condition observed by anyone. But this view is also defective. Thus, Ayer, too, could not satisfactorily solve the problems pertaining to perception.

The fifth chapter of my book is 'The Problem of Self.' In accordance with his aim of the demonstration of the meaninglessness of all metaphysics, Ayer eliminates the transcendental existence of the self too. Like Hume, Ayer also rejects the possibility of the self as a metaphysical entity. For him, a self is a logical construction out of sense-experiences. But whereas in Hume's account, a self is an aggregate of sense-experiences, or sense-experiences which constitute a particular self are parts of it. In Ayer's view, "self is reducible to sense-experiences, in the sense that to say anything about the self is always to say something about sense-experiences."[12] A sense-experience is, according to him, a whole composed of sense-contents. All things are logical construction out of sense-contents. Therefore, the self is also a logical construction. He defines sense content as a part of sense-experience. But in saying that 'an object is a logical construction out of sense contents,' sense-contents are not parts but elements of logical construction.

This assertion expresses a syntactical fact that sentences referring to an object are translatable into sentences referring to sense contents. According to him an object is distinguished from other objects by reason that "it is constituted by different sense contents or by sense-contents differently related." The words mental and physical belong to objects which are logical constructions out of sense-contents, but sense-contents themselves are neither mental nor physical.

Since he analyses mind and body as things, the problem concerning mind-body relation is fictitious or a pesudo-problem, which arises out of the meaningless metaphysical conceptions of mind and body, or mind and matter as substances. He considers the question, can a sense content occur in the sense history of more than one single self? His answer is, it cannot, because sense experiences are constituted by sense-contents and "for any two sense experiences to belong to the sense history of the same it is necessary and sufficient that they should contain organic sense contents which are elements of the same body." But it is logically impossible for any organic sense content to be an element of more than one body."

All organic sense contents are private by reason of the fact that any organic sense content cannot be an element of more than one body. A distinction which Ayer draws between mind and matter is that "a privacy which is denied to matter is attributed to mind." He uses the word 'private' in the sense in which thoughts, feelings, dreams, imaginings, sensation and memories are private. These are the things to which one alone has access. One can communicate them to others, but cannot transfer them. But physical objects or events are not private. Different people do perceive the same physical object, and thus it is public.

Here Ayer clearly remarks that this distinction is purely linguistic. But this analysis of the self leads to solipsism. Ayer himself was aware of this objection, so he makes an attempt to avoid it on the ground that this objection contradicts the basic assumption of his analysis. His analysis of the self is not restricted only to oneself but it considers other selves also. He interprets the experiences of others in terms of their bodily behaviour. Hume attempted to define personal identity with the help of memory. But memory, according to both Ayer and Hume, cannot be a satisfactory principle. A person bears not only those experiences which he is able to remember but also those which he fails to remember. Besides this, in claiming that an experience is remembered it is already pre-supposed that it is mine. It follows from this that memory itself presupposes personal identity.

Though with the help of memory personal identity cannot be defined but as of Hume, Ayer too maintains that memory produces self-consciousness. "For" he says, "all that is involved in self-consciousness is the ability of a self to remember some of its earlier states."[13] But this view is objectionable as it fail to explain one's present experience. Memory involves a consciousness of merely one's past experiences. When I say 'I am sitting now in the chair' it will be absurd to suggest that I am talking of my past experience. To face this difficulty Ayer in his later work explains self-consciousness in the way that "to be thinking about a problem, or remembering some event, or seeing or hearing something, or deciding to do something, or feeling some emotion, such as jealousy or fear, entails being conscious."[14] Though this is also open to criticisms.

Ayer defines personal identity in terms of bodily identity and bodily identity in terms of resemblance and continuity of experience. According to him, the criterian that determines the identity of his body. And different bodily states, in his view, are spatio-temporarily related. Ayer's view of the self is no less objectionable. Several arguments have been given against his view.

The last chapter of my thesis is 'A Critical Evaluation.' The intention of logical empiricists, as Ayer himself maintains, is to purify philosophy of metaphysics and develop it as a branch of logic. Thus they claim that philosophy is not a special study of speculations, but it is an enquiry into language. They identify philosophy with linguistic analysis. But is this identification legitimate? Can philosophy be identified with logic or linguistic? Linguistic analysis is, of course, an important instrument in the way of clarifying confusions. And all the philosophers make use of this method of analysis. But philosophy is an investigation of truth and reality. It cannot be identified with linguistics or logic.

Language has its own limits and a philosopher, in any true investigation, must realise its limitations. Philosophical analysis is done by thought and thought involves language, but on account of this philosophy cannot be identified with linguistic analysis. Language is secondary to philosophy; it is only a means. Logical empiricists attempt to demolish to metaphysical speculations by claiming that its propositions are "pseudo propositions." They are meaningless nonsensical propositions. A meaningful proposition consists of meaningful words and these words are in accordance with the rules of syntax. Metaphysical propositions are meaningless because logical empiricists claim that they either contain meaningless words of if words are meaningful they are discordant with the rules of syntax.

According to logical empiricists, propositions of existential import have an exclusively empirical reference and this empirical reference can be conclusively shown by logical analysis. They formulate principle of verification according to which a proposition is meaningful if it is either analytic or empirically verifiable. First of all this distinction of analytic and empirical proposition is criticised as it involves several difficulties. Ayer does not make this distinction, as Kant made, on the ground whether a proposition extends the knowledge which we have or fails to extend it. If a proposition fails to extend the knowledge then it is analytic, and if it extends the knowledge it is synthetic or empirical. By calling a proposition analytic Kant never meant that it gives no knowledge, but only that it does not extend knowledge. Ayer disapproves this way of making distinction by remarking that an analytic proposition is factually empty because it is tautology. He defines analyticity in terms of synonymity.

But Ayer himself fails to show the analyticity of those propositions which he himself regards as analytic by this definition. If analyticity is defined in terms of synonmity, if an analytic proposition is nothing but a tautology then his proposition 'Either some ants are parasite or none are 'which he holds analytic is not analytic as a proposition 'An oculist is an eye doctor' is analytic. For the former does not have a pair of synonymous symbols as the later proposition has. In fact, his definition of analyticity is not satisfactory as he could not explain the analyticity of all analytic propositions. He has no clear conception as to why an analytic proposition is factually empty and how can it be defined in terms of synonymity.

Even granted this distinction of analytic and synthetic propositions, Ayer's thesis is not acceptable. According to him any scientific use of language must be the utterance of either a tautology or an empirical statement, this is what the verification principle in effect asserted. But, then, the question is, what is the status of the verification principle itself? It is hard to maintain that the verification principle is either analytic or empirically verifiable. If it is maintained as analytic, it would be nothing more than tautology and from tautologies no conclusion can follow. If it is empirical, then the principle itself would require verification. The claim that the meaning of a proposition consists in its verification is, in fact, indefinite. It involves the fallacy of infinite regress for verification principle itself requires verification and again that verification would require verification, and there is no end to this process.

Ayer refutes all metaphysics, ethics, aesthetics and religion because their propositions are neither scientific propositions nor tautologies. It is legitimate to assert that their propositions are not empirically verifiable but because of this reason they cannot be claimed as meaningless. Empirical criterion is not the only criterion to judge the meaning of all proposition. Spiritual realizations, introspection, ethical and aesthetic experiences are higher experiences. These experiences are not sensuous but intuitive and therefore they can not be verified empirically; they are experienced only by intuition. After rejecting all metaphysical speculations, Ayer explains his own thesis of logical empiricism. In his view, "experience has to be rich enough to furnish the entire world." Accordingly he explains all mind and matter, space and time, appearance and reality as logical constructions out of sense-experiences.

To solve the problem of perception, he explains the perceiving subject, that is mind or self, and the object of perception as logical constructions out of sense-experiences. The act of perception is explained by the indirect theory of perception. We do not perceive physical objects directly; what we directly perceive are sense data. But this explanation of the theory of perception cannot be accepted. If it is maintained that in order to perceive a physical objective we have first to perceive sense-data, it brings besides physical objects, the existence of curious objects called sense data. To avoid this difficulty Ayer holds that the introduction of the terminology of sense-data is not the introduction of a new class of entities besides physical objects. When he says that an object is a logical construction out of sense-data, what he means is simply that a statement about physical object is equivalent to or translatable into the statement about sense-data. But even then he fails to provide a satisfactory of perception.

Though Ayer denies that sense-data are objects like the physical objects and yet he asserts that sense data are what we immediately experience. But then immediate experiences are to be included in the inventory of existents as of physical objects. And if they are also existents, as of physical objects, then to perceive them some other sense-data would be required. It is for this reason that sometimes such an interpretation of the theory of perception is characterized as a logical howler.

Ayer explains both the perceiving subject, i.e. self or mind, and the physical object as logical constructions out of sense-data. The question very naturally arises whether sense-data are mental or physical. If they are former the later cannot be constructed out of them. To answer such questions, Ayer adopts the view of 'neutral monism.' Sense-data are neither mental nor physical, they are raw material out of which both mental and physical objects are constructed. But then the difficulty arises as to having to distinguish a mental object from a physical object. How is the self distinguished from matter or a physical object? According to Ayer, there is no fundamental distinction between mental and physical objects, for they both are logical constructions. The distinction is of secondary importance. One object or one logical construction is distinguished from another on the ground that they are constituted by different sense contents of by sense-contents differently related. But by this interpretation.

Ayer could not solve the problem of mind-body relation, self-consciousness, one's knowledge of other minds and personal identity. In his view, self is a logical construction out of sense-experiences, and a physical object, like pen, is a logical construction out of sense-content. A sense-content, according to him, is a part of sense experience. It follows from this that a sense-experience and a sense-contents re not one and the same thing. A whole is distinguished from its parts. Accordingly, to say that a self is a logical construction out of sense-experience is quite different from saying that a pen is a logical construction out of sense-contents. And if self and a physical object, or mind and body are different, one should explain the relation between these different entities. Ayer's explanation of the mind-body problem, by saying that there is no basic differences between them for they both are logical constructions, is, somehow, not satisfactory. Ayer analyses the notion of self-consciousness by believing that thinking, remembering seeing or hearing or feeling entail being conscious, but this analysis is also objectionable. According to Ayer, the self is a logical construction out of sense-experiences. If self-consciousness is interpreted in such a way, what is that which does thinking about a problem or remembering some events, or seeing or hearing something or feeling some emotion? Does a sense content think or remember, or feel anything? Ayer could not explain this problem too.

The problem of one's knowledge of other minds is solved by Ayer in terms of bodily behaviour, but this interpretation is also defective. Ayer reduces the experience of other persons to their bodily behaviour and bodily behaviour in terms of sense content. And this reduction of the sense-content is extended to the bodily identity. Sense contents, according to him, are private, in the sense that a sense-content cannot be an element of more than one body. But if sense-contents are private, then the intersubjective observability of bodies of other persons would be abandoned. And if it is maintained that bodies are inter subjectively observable then they must be defined in terms of public sense-contents. But it would be self contradictory to say that sense-contents are public. Similarly his explanation of the problem of personal identity is unsatisfactory.

He feels that personal identity cannot be defined in terms of experience, as Hume tried to define it, for there is no general principle of experience. Ayer avoids this difficulty by defining personal identity in terms or bodily identity. He resolves the difficulty of uniting different bodily states of a person by the spatio-temporal continuity. But here it is to be noted that he rejected Humes's view of personal identity on the same ground. Thus his own explanation of personal identity is also rejected, for there is no general principle of uniting different bodily states. The spacio-temporal continuity does not make any advance over the difficulty of Hume.

In his enthusiasm for the clarification of the terminology of science and philosophy through the elimination of all metaphysical speculations with the help of linguistic analysis, Ayer commits himself to linguistic solipsism. He explains all things as logical constructions; but if all things, the self and the not-self, the mind and the matter, or myself, otherselves, and physical objects are nothing but logical constructions, such questions are raised. How is this construction possible? Who constructs these different objects? Ayer has failed to give any satisfactory answer of these questions.

The present book is a study on Analysis of Great Philosophers with special reference on the philosophy of A.J. Ayer in the context of contemporary movement of logical empiricism. The study is a modest attempt at an understanding and analysis of the basic problems of philosophy involved in the empiricism of Ayer. I have also attempted to evaluate the merits and demerits of Ayer's thought in propagating the cause of empiricism in the twentieth century.

REFERENCES

1. Tractataus, 4.003.
2. *Ibid.*, 4.0031.
3. Wittgenstein, Philosophical Investigations, para 109, p. 47.
4. Ayer, Language, Truth and Logic, p. 26.
5. Ayer, The Concept of a Person, p. 3.
6. *Ibid.*,p. 5.
7. *Ibid.*, p. 11.
8. Ayer, Language, Truth and Logic, p. 32.
9. Herbert Feigl, Logical Empiricism, in Herbert Feigl. and Wilferd Sellar's Readings in philosophical Analysis, p. 12.
10. *Ibid.*, p. 6.
11. *Ibid.*, p. 11.
12. Ayer, Language Truth and Logic, p. 128.
13. Ayer, Language, Truth and Logic, p. 126.
14. Ayer, The Concept of a Person, p. 82.

2

The Nature of Philosophical Analysis

I

Logical empiricists claim that philosophy is to be identified with analysis. "Analysis is the one and only legitimate activity of philosophers."[1] They maintain that philosophy is not a doctrine but an activity. A.J. Ayer writes, "It would surely be advisable for us to abandon the term 'philosophy' altogether as a name for a distinctive branch of knowledge, and invent some new description for the activity which we were minded to call the activity of philosophizing."[2] And the activity of philosophizing is essentially analysis.

Now the question is what do they claim to analyse? As in his Construction and Analysis Strawson asks "Was it, for example, sentences, of the indicative or assertive kind? Or was it the meanings of those sentences by some, rather unhappily called propositions? Or was it the thoughts or beliefs which the sentences expressed? Or the statements they were used to make?" And he himself gives the answer, "Analysis of sentences suggests the grammarian, analysis of thoughts or beliefs, the psychologist, and analysis of statements, perhaps the policeman or the advocate. May be it is best to say that the objects of analysis were propositions."[3] Philosophers claim to analyse propositions. A proposition itself is neither a statement or a sentence nor is it a judgement, but it is expressed in the form of a sentence, judgement or statement. Thus if a sentence or a statement is meaningful, it expresses genuine proposition.

Philosophy is a special branch of knowledge. It is peculiar only by its method, i.e. the method of analysis. Ayer, in the very first line of his book, The Problem of Knowledge, writes,[1] "It is by its method rather than its subject matter that philosophy is distinguished from other arts or sciences." Every branch of knowledge has its own method of analysis peculiar to its subject matter. Philosophy differs from other arts or sciences only by its method of analysis. Philosophical analysis is neither analysis as used in science nor is it of the type of analysis as of common sense. Philosophers make statements which are intended to be true, and they commonly rely on arguments both to support their own theories and to refute the theories of others. These philosophical arguments are peculiar in their character and they differ from science or mathematics. For neither the proof of a philosophical statement consists in formal demonstration, as of mathematical statement, nor it is tested by observation as of the descriptive sciences. "They are neutral with respect to particular matters of fact." The function of science is to describe 'what is fact'? and the function of Philosophy is to analyse 'what do we mean by fact?' Ayer writes, "What is in dispute in such cases is not whether, in a given set of circumstances, this or that event will happen, but rather how anything at all that happens is to be described."[3] The philosopher, as an analyst, is not directly concerned with the properties of things. He is concerned only with the way in which we speak about them.

Philosophical propositions are not factual but linguistic. They do not describe the behaviour of any physical or mental events but they merely express their definitions. Philosophers ask such questions as, 'What is mind'? 'What is truth'? 'What is good'? and so on. It does not mean that they do not know the common usage of these words or expressions. Indeed, in doing so, they seek to give an analysis of their meaning. There is a difference between 'the use of an expression' and 'analysis of its meaning.' As an example, Ayer takes the case of 'Knowledge.' In the dictionary we see that the verb 'to know' is used in many ways. Such definitions which a dictionary gives are 'to be aware of or appraised of, 'to apprehend or comprehend as fact or truth' and so on. "To possess the information which the dictionary provides about the accredited uses of the English word 'to know' or the corresponding words in other languages is no doubt a necessary qualification for giving an analysis of knowledge but it is not sufficient."[4] A philosopher requires something more which is not required by a lexicographer. After having all information philosophers still ask, 'What is knowledge'? and then they seek to give an analysis of its meaning.

Thus philosophical analysis is essentially the study of language, but it is quite different from that of other important studies of language. Although linguists, philologists, grammarians, lexicographers, etc. are also involved in a study of language, but philosophical analysis must not be confused with them. For whereas other studies of language deal with scientific questions, such as, how we use our language; what meanings words have; how languages begin, change and die, etc. They are interested in discovering facts about these scientific questions. And these scientific questions about language can be answered only through the use of the scientific method. But the analytic philosopher does not study language in order to formulate such scientific hypotheses about it, because such a study of language is an invaluable tool for him to achieve his primary goal of settling philosophical questions.

But analytic philosophy is not 'homogeneous and monolithic'. Ammerman writes, "There is no single philosophy of analysis. There is no analytic 'party line', no heresies, no pontifical authorities. The word analysis is used here as a way of grouping together a number of heterogeneous philosophers who share certain interests and procedures."[5]

II

In 1921, Wittgenstein wrote, "Philosophy aims at the logical clarification of thought. Philosophy is not a doctrine but an activity."[2] Within a few years this view was widely circulated. It was adopted by logical empiricists and it developed in the form of linguistic movement. Thus analysis has come to occupy an important place in the twentieth century philosophy. But Analysis as the method of philosophy or the idea of the clarification of thoughts is nothing new. Analysis has always played an important role in the development of philosophical thought. Since the time of Plato all the great philosophers made use of the method of analysis in order to provide a solution of intricate philosophical problems and also in order to being clarity in thinking. Socrates was primarily concerned to answer such question as 'What is justice'?, 'What is knowledge'? etc. It may be asked whether this is the only aim that philosophy can legitimately have. Why should it be so restricted?" Ayer says "the reason is that all other avenues of knowledge are thought to be already pre-empted. A philosopher is directed to conceptual or linguistic analysis, as the only field which they can profitably explore. This conceptual or linguistic analysis is also not new. Ayer himself remarks that it is already implicit in the famous passage of Hume with which the concludes his book An Enquiry Concerning Human Understanding. Hume writes, 'When we run over libraries, persuaded of these principles, what havoc must we make? If we take in our hand any volume of divinity or school metaphysics, for instance, let us ask, does it contain any abstract reasoning concerning quantity and number? No. Does it contain any experimental reasoning concerning matter of fact and experience? No. Commit it then to the flames: for it can contain nothing but sophistry and illusion."[7] Accordingly to Ayer, there are some shortcomings in the arguments of Hume. "He does not apply his criterion to his own philosophy, but he most probably regarded it as coming within the domain of experimental reasoning..... It is not to be expected that Hume should have distinguished the subject matter of his Treatise of Human Nature or his Enquiry Concerning Human Understanding from what we should nowadays call psychology. His main business is with concepts, which he is indeed concerned not only to analyse but also to harness to the profit of his scepticism."[8]

Although logical empiricists criticize Hume on some points, but, in fact, they are greatly influenced by him. As Ayer himself admits that the assumptions on which Hume was relying were taken up by the logical positivists and embodied in what came to be known as the principle of verifiability or the verification principle. This principle is expressed in the famous slogan that "the meaning of a proposition is its method of verification."[9] But it was not only Hume who had this credit, before Hume the credit goes to Locke and Berkeley too. For Locke, epistemology should be the starting point and centre of all philosophical discussion. In his famous work An Essay Concerning Human Understanding. Locke writes,[10] before we set ourselves upon inquiries of that nature, it was necessary to examine our abilities, and see what objects our understanding were or were not fitted to deal with. In response to this challenge, he wrote his An Essay Concerning Human Understanding in order to discover what is the origin of our ideas, to show what is the certainty, the evidence, and the extent of our knowledge, to compel philosophy to abandon what surpasses human comprehension by making the limits of its capacity.

In his view, language is the 'great instrument' of knowledge. 'Words' and 'ideas' are closely connected. Locke devoted himself to the purely analytic tasks of definite knowledge and classifying propositions, and displaying the nature of material things.

After Locke it was Berkeley whose revolutionary philosophy of language for the first time systematically challenged the traditional assumption that all words are or should be used as signs of our ideas of things, and that any significant discourse must be regarded as a statement of fact about the nature of things. Berkeley never denied the reality of material things but he denied "the adequacy of Locke's analysis of the notion of a material thing. He maintained that to say of various "ideas of sensation" that they belonged to a single material thing was not, as Locke thought, to say they were related to a single unobservable underlying 'somewhat' but rather that they stood in certain relations to one another."[11] On this point Ayer agrees with Berkeley. But Ayer points out that he committed the mistake of supposing that what was immediately given in sensation was necessarily mental. Berkeley criticized Locke because he asserted the existence of unobservable underlying entity of 'somewhat'. But he also asserted the existence of 'God' as a cause of ideas which is also an unobservable entity. Ayer writes, "He must be criticized also for falling to see that the argument which he uses to dispose of Locke's analysis of a material thing is fatal to his own conception of the nature of the self, a point which was effectively seized upon by Hume."[14]

Hume found that it is all due to the 'theory of causation' that Locke believed in 'somewhat' or Berkeley believed in 'God'. Thus Hume criticized the theory of causation itself. He affirmed that all events seem entirely loose and separate. One event follows another; but we never can observe any tie between them. They are conjoined, but never connected. According to Hume, we call the one object, Cause; the other, Effect. We suppose that there is some connection between them; some power in the one, by which it infallibly produces the other, and operates with the greatest certainty and strongest necessity. But there is nothing in a number of instances .... except only that after a repetition of similar instances, the mind is carried by habit, upon the appearance of one event, to except its usual attendant, and to believe that it will exist. Hume asserted that "the necessity is something, that exists in the mind, not in objects; nor is it possible for us ever to form the most distant idea of it, considered as a quality in bodies.[15] Though Hume does not actually put forward any view concerning the nature of philosophical propositions themselves, but those of his works which are commonly accounted philosophical are, apart from certain passages which deal with questions of psychology, works of analysis.

Although English empiricism has great importance in the development of philosophical analysis as it is foreshadowed by the writings of empiricist philosophers, but "it was Russell and Moore primarily, around the turn of the century, who challenged decisively the predominant philosophical views of the period and took the first giant steps toward a new conception of philosophy."[16] Ayer and Urmson[17] also regard Russell and Moore as the co-founders of the movement of analysis. They were against idealism, but they were not in complete agreement as to what is wrong with idealism. Though idealism was rejected by philosophers before Russell and Moore, but, before Moore there was no philosopher who had concentrated his critical attack with such intensity upon the meanings of the metaphysical propositions which were advanced by the Idealists.

Though Russell has had a greater influence than Moore, not only in the world at large, but also through his purely philosophical writings, it was Moore who was chiefly responsible for the restriction of philosophy to an analysis. Analysis plays an important role in determining the character of Moore's philosophical views. Moore is a common sense and ordinary language philosopher. Accordingly his method of analysis is based upon common sense appeals and ordinary everyday language. He uses analysis not for the discovery of 'new facts' about the universe but for the clarification of the concepts.

In 'A Reply to his Critics' Moore makes his position clear regarding the nature of analysis. In his usage, he says, "both analysandum and analysans must be concepts or propositions, not merely verbal expressions."[18] Analysandum is what is to be analyzed and analysans is which does the analyzing. He gives several examples of what he calls analysis. Firstly, "The concept 'being a brother' is identical with the concept 'being a male sibling'." For him in making this assertion, he is giving a correct analysis of this concept. In another way he gives the same analysis of the same concept by saying that the propositional function 'X is a brother' is identical with the propositional function 'X is a male sibling'. There is also a way in which the same analysis may be given by saying that to say a person is a brother is the same thing as to say that the person is a male sibling."

Another salient feature of Moore's analysis is his defence

of common sense. Common sense believes that there are in the Universe, at least two different kinds of things, there are, to begin with, enormous numbers of material objects; and there are also a very great number of mental acts of consciousness. Commonsense believes that both material objects and acts of consciousness are in space and time. Moore affirms that all material objects at any given moment, situated somewhere or other in something which we call space.

Likewise all material objects, and all the acts of consciousness of ourselves and other animals upon the earth, are in time. Moore's refutation of idealism is based upon the commonsense view of the world. He refutes the internality of relations which is accepted by the idealists in one way or another. He holds that "some relations are purely external" and that "in the case of many relational properties which things have, the fact that they have them is a mere matter of fact; that the things in question might have existed without having them. That this, which seems obvious, is true, seems to me to be the most important thing that can be meant by saying that some relations are purely external." Thus the basic idealist principle is false because it 'flies in the face of common sense.'[19]

But according to Ayer the view of common sense 'over simplifies the position both of the empirical and the formal sciences, there is in fact no universal agreement among metaphysicians as to what constitutes a valid proof .... Neither is there universal agreement among physicists of biologists as to the states of their theories." Ayer argues, "there is, of course, a very large measure of agreement, but it does not go all the way. For example, some mathematicians will accept a reduction and absurdum argument as proof of the existence of a number which satisfies such and such a function, other will attribute existence only to those numbers which they can positively construct."[20] Another radical defect is that the distinction between knowing the truth of a proposition and knowing the analysis is not so sharp as the argument is required. Moreover, common sense has no definite meaning. As it changes under the influence of science, though the change is not always immediately apparent. We still speak of the notion of the sun, of its rising in the east and setting in the west, but the meaning of these words, at least to educated people, is not what it was before the acceptance of Copernican theory.[21] Thus the aim of philosophical analysis, i.e. to give a definite description is not fulfilled by Moore's version.

Bertrand Russell is another important philosopher of the analytic movement. Mr. Morris Weitz writes, "The fundamental event in his philosophy is the method of analysis."[22] Although Russell and Moore are regarded as the co-founders of analytic movement, but their methods of analysis are different from one another. Russell was greatly influenced by logic and mathematics. In his philosophy analysis comes in the form of 'theory of discription'. By a discription' he means "a phrase of the form the so and so or of some equivalent form." In his Introduction to Mathematical Philosophy, he asserts that a description may be of two sorts, definite and indefinite (or ambiguous). An indefinite description is a phrase of the form 'a so - and - so', and a definite description is a phrase of the form 'the so and so' (in the singular). In philosophical analysis, by the term 'description' he means 'definite description' a phrase of the form 'the so and so'. His assumption is that the meaning of a name is to be identified with the object which the name denotes. ... Anything that could be mentioned was said by him to be a term : any term could be a logical subject of a proposition; and anything that could be the logical subject of a proposition could be named. This is his 'theory of description.' By this supposition idealism was automatically rejected because, it followed that one could in principle use names to refer not only to any particular thing that exists at any place and time, but also to abstract entities of all sorts, to non-existent things like the present Tsar of Russia, to mythological entities like the Cyclops, even to logically impossible entities like the greatest prime number. Thus Russell refuted the theory of idealism in his own way.

But there are some defects in Russell's views. As Ayer points out, "An important consequence of the theory of description is that existence is treated as a property of propositional functions."[23] In an article, Is Existence a Predicate? Moore argues that "one can significantly say of the object to which the demonstrative is being used to refer that it might not have existed. But to say that this might not have existed is to imply that the proposition 'This does not exist' might have been true, from which it follows that the sentence "This does not exist' must be significant. But if the sentence 'This does not exist' is significant, it expresses a false proposition. Consequently the proposition that this exists is a true proposition, and from this it follows that the sentence 'This exists' is also significant."[24] Here Ayer does agree with Moore. He asserts that he thinks that this argument is valid, and that Russell is therefore mistaken in believing that existence should always be constructed as a property of propositional functions. Ayer points put another defect in Russell and holds that it does not give an accurate account of the way in which definite descriptive phrases are actually used.[25]

But in spite of these criticisms its philosophical importance can not be denied. For Ayer, "one of the great merits of his theory of descriptions is that it does throw light upon the use of a certain class of expressions in ordinary speech, and that this is a point of philosophical importance."[26] Thus for Russell and Moore analysis, whether by means of the techniques of symbolic logic or by an appeal to ordinary language, was primarily an instrument to sharpen and clarify philosophical problems. Ammerman says, "The writings of Russell and Moore were to prepare the ground for the next more extreme phase of the revolution."[27]

Ludwig Wittgenstein is the first analyst who argues the more extreme thesis that metaphysical questions are not questions at all. They are from their very nature unanswerable. In his Tractatus, Wittgenstein argues that most of the propositions and questions to be found in philosophical works are not false but nonsensical. Consequently we cannot give any answer to questions of this kind, but can only establish that they are nonsensical. — And it is not surprising that the deepest problems are in fact not problems at all.[28] Wittgenstein divides all meaningful propositions into tautologies, contradictions and propositions (by propositions, he means, true or false empirical propositions). He writes, "Propositions show what they say: tautologies and contradictions show that they say nothing.

A tautology has no truth conditions, since it is unconditionally true: and a contradiction is true on no condition.

Tautologies and contradictions lacksense."[29]

"The sense of a proposition is its agreement or disagreement with possibilities of existence and non-existence of state of affairs."[30] Thus, Wittegenstein asserts, "A tautology's truth is certain, a proposition's possible, a contradiction's impossible."[31]

Although logical empiricism was not exclusively an outgrowth of Wittgenstein, some ideas of Wittgenstein's Tractatus re-endorsed by logical empiricists. Regarding the method of analysis, it is clearly assumed that he used this method only for the removal of misunderstanding, whereas logical empiricists use analysis not for removal of cramps but for the clarification of conceptual confusions too.

Warnock, in his article entitled Analysis and Imagination,[32] following Strawson, divides analysis into therapeutic and systematic. Therapeutic analysis, as the title shows, cures the mind of its afflicting puzzles. Wittgenstein is the exponent of this type of analysis. According to him, "philosophy is a battle against the bewitchment of our intelligence by means of language."[33]

Systematic analysis describes concepts and speech-forms systematically. The analysis of logical empiricists is mainly systematic, although it is at the same time therapeutic, as it attempts to undu the knots of our thinking.

III

All logical empiricists are united in saying that all

metaphysical propositions are meaningless. On this point they agree with Wittgenstein that metaphysical questions are unanswerable, for they are not questions at all. All meaningful propositions are either (1) analytic or formal propositions, or (2) empirically verifiable. The proposition which cannot verify even in principle are devoid of sense. Such propositions are called "pseudo-propositions." Rudolf Carnap, one of the major figures of logical empiricism, defines metaphysical propositions in such a way that they claim to represent knowledge about something which is over or beyond all experience.

Ayer claims that "the practice of analysis should be the starting point for philosophy."[34] Though, as we have seen, "practice covers quite a number of activities, which differ from one another either in their methods or their aims or both."[35] Ayer distinguishes several of them, but he does not claim that "this is the only way in which they could reasonably be classified. In many respects, they shade into one another and it is a fairly arbitrary matter where one draws the lines between them."[36]

The first type of analysis, is formal analysis, which, according to Ayer, is led by F.P. Ramsay. In his The Foundations of Mathematics he writes, "In philosophy we take the propositions we make in science and everyday life, and try to exhibit them in a logical system with primitive terms and definitions, etc. Essentially, philosophy is a system of definitions, or only too often a description of how definition might be given."[37] For the formal analysis the function of philosophy is to give formal definitions of particular concepts. And it has played an important role in science and everyday life. "Sometimes a term which is not used univocally in ordinary speech is resolved into terms with different senses, and an attempt is made by formal methods to define each of them precisely. This has happened in the case of the concept of probability."[38] Ayer says, "It may be that the ordinary use of such a term is too loose for these definitions to capture is exactly in all its variations, but the aim is not so much to give an accurate account of ordinary usage as to clarify and, if necessary, sharpen concepts in a way that will increase their utility to science.[39] He takes an example of Einstein's definition of Simultaneity, "one could say that it brought to light implications to our use of the term which had previously escaped our notice; but it would probably be more correct to say that Einstein in his Theory of Relativity showed the ordinary concept of simultaneity to be defective and refined it."[40] There is another example of Hume's definition of causality, "the interest lies, not in Hume's actual definition, which is hardly acceptable in the form in which he presents it, but in the arguments which lead him to it."[41] Thus philosophers give definitions in order to refine the concepts of science and everyday discourse.

The second type of analysis is that in which "philosophers are concerned for the most part not just to clarify these distinctions but also to account for them; to consider how far they are forced upon us either by the nature of our experience or by the requirements of successful communication."[42] Here again clarification or definition is not sufficient, but justification is also needed. In this type of practice of analysis, analysts ask the question such as "Philosophers talk of indicative sentences as expressing propositions, but what are propositions? Do we have to conceive of them as abstract entities, existing independently of the sentences which express them"?[43] They explain that propositions are distinguished from one another in different ways, they may be simple propositions or compound propositions. Compound propositions are also differed themselves; they may be truth-functional propositions in the sense that their truth value is determined by the truth-value of their components. Clearly the truth value of a truth functional proposition either it is in the form of conjunctive proposition as 'p and q' or in the form of disjunctive proposition as 'p or q' wholly depends on the truth value of its components 'p' and 'q'. If the conjunction is true, both conjuncts must be true, if the disjunction is true either of the disjuncts must be true. But, "on the other hand" Ayer says, "many hypothetical propositions appear not to be true-functional. For instance, the validity of the proposition 'If I had struck this match, it would have lit' seems not be affected by the falsity of its antecedent clause. But then the question how such propositions are validated presents a difficult problem."[44]

Ayer discusses another important class of international expression which "consists of those that introduce modality, in the sense that they serve to characterize propositions not just as true or false, but as possible, necessary, or impossible,"[45] They are intentional in the sense that "some but not all type propositions are held to be necessary, and some but not all false propositions to be impossible."[46] Ayer says, "This doubt extends to the distinction between analytic and synthetic propositions, with which the distinction between the necessary and the contingent is sometimes held to coincide. Again, the argument is that the notion of meaning is not sufficiently clear for us to be justified in accepting the characterization of analytic propositions as those which are true solely in virtue of the meaning of the signs which express them."[47] He says, "there are philosophers who accept both the distinction between necessary and contingent and that between analytic and synthetic propositions, but do not treat them as coincident. Some, following Kant, believe that the propositions of pure mathematics, though necessary cannot be shown to be analytic in any accepted sense of this term, and some believe also that scientific laws exhibit what they call natural necessity. It is in this way that they distinguish generalizations of law from generalizations of fact."[48]

Here Ayer makes it clear that he does not mean to say that "they are merely verbal in a sense that might be taken to imply that they were trivial. Apart from their intrinsic interest, there examination throws light not only on the workings of our language but also on the character of the world which it serves to describe."[49]

Another type of analysis is the analysis of ordinary usage. This is a type of informal analysis. The leader of the analysis of ordinary usage was J.L. Austin. The function of Philosophy for him is to analyse the language which is spoken by ordinary people. Austin gives an example of different types of speech act. "The natural language which these philosophers studied was English, and what they termed ordinary usage was the usage of educated English-speakers like themselves. This gave some of their works a rather limited interest, but some of it had a more general application. Thus, one of Austin's achievements was to determinate a class of what he called performative statements. These are statements which do not so much report activities as help to bring them about."[50] He takes some examples, "the judge who says to a convicted criminal 'You will go to prison for six months' is not thereby making a prediction; he is carrying out a ritual performance of which the man's going to prison is the probable effect. To say 'I promise' under the appropriate conditions is not just to report that one is making a promise but actually to make it."[51]

Ayer writes, "The fashion for ordinary language philosophy, during the comparatively short period that it existed in any strength, generated more heat on either side than now seems to have been warranted."[52] It can be said in its defence that "there is no way of investigating concepts except as they are embodied in some languages; if one is going to investigate some language, it is desirable to understand it thoroughly, and the language which one understands best is likely to be one's own."[53] But, "on the other hand, not all linguistic distinctions are of philosophical interest, and if the practitioners of this type of analysis had a weakness it was that they paid too much attention to niceties of English usage which had no discernible bearing on any thing that any philosopher had ever regarded as a problem."[54]

There are some other analysts like Wittgenstein for whom also analysis comes in the category of informal analysis, but they have a pecularity of their own inspite of a lot of similarity between Wittgenstein's analysis and the analysis of ordinary usage. In the analysis of ordinary usage a philosopher is concerned with language in use, and Wittgenstein also says that "the meaning of a word is its use in the language."[55]

Wittgenstein speaks of "language games." As there are

some rules in the games, every language must have some rules. According to him 'Every sentence in our language is "in order as it is".'[56] He says, "Philosophy may in no way interfere with the actual use of language; it can in the end only describe it."[57] Ayer says, "theoretically at least, though not so much in practice, he goes even further than the analysis of ordinary usage in limiting the scope of philosophical analysis."[58] He writes, "Where Wittgenstein chiefly differs from the analysts of ordinary usage is that he has little or no interest in usage as such. His descriptions of it are framed with a view to resolving philosophical problems, which he sees above all as sources of perplexity."[59] Wittgenstein admits that the problems are solved, not by giving new information, but by arranging what we have always known. Philosophy is a battle against the bewitchment of our intelligence by means of language.[60] Ayer comments that "our intelligence becomes bewitched, not when we actually use our language to talk about the world, in the straight forward way we mostly do, but when we start reflecting on the way we use it. We make mistakes such as that of supposing that all words function like names, or that the things to which the same words applies must all possess one common quality, whereas there may be no more than what Wittgenstein calls a 'family resemblance' between them."[61]

Gilbert Ryle is another notable philosopher of the informal analysis. According to Ayer "in his book The concept of Mind, the main object of which is to discredit the duaslistic conception of mind and body, vividly characterized by Ryle as the myth of the ghost in the machine, he attempts, among other things, to show the volitions are mythical, and one way in which he does this is by drawing attention to the fact that the mental processes which words like 'willing' might be thought to name simply do not occur."[62] Thus these philosophers use analysis to prove that there is no mysterious entity. Metaphysical propositions are not concerned with facts but they are due to the faulty use of language.

Sometimes the practice of analysis is concerned with the theory of knowledge. In this, it has three main purpose: "to arrive at a satisfactory definition of knowledge; to determine what sorts of propositions can be known to be true; and to explain how these propositions can be known to be true."[63] According to Ayer the first of these aims is relatively unimportant. For it is of no great consequence exactly where one draws the line between knowledge and true belief. He writes, "The practice has most commonly been to start with propositions of such a sort that one can be certain, or virtually certain, of their truth, and then see what further propositions they can be supposed to justify."[64] Descartes was the originator of this procedure. Ayer says, "Descartes envisaged a malicious demon who had the power to cause us to mistake false propositions for true ones, and then sought to discover whether there was any proposition which one could not be mistaken in believing. His answer is that I cannot be mistaken in believing that I exist, since my denial or even doubt of my own existence itself implies it."[65] But this method is criticised. Ayer says, "It might be objected that if the demon were all powerful, he could cause us to be mistaken even about the validity of such a deductive arguments. And if we are entitled to trust our intuition in this case, why not in others where we appear to face the alternative of accepting some proposition or failing into self contradiction?"[66] He admits that "Descartes does not allow the demon to be all powerful. His power is limited by the role for which he is cast, since he is required to deceive a person who is already assumed to exist. He could still delude me into thinking that I do not exist when I do, if such a thought is possible by not ex hypothesi into thinking that I exist when I do not. In short, Descartes assumed his own existence in order to infer it."[67] Ayer says, "He assumed the existence only of his mind and not his body, and even so he may be held to have gone too far, in respect of what was strictly deducible from his avowed premiss. For he took himself to be a thinking substance, enduring through a period of time, and, as his critics have pointed out, this cannot be deduced from the occurence of a momentary thought. Even if the substance is not credited with any temporal duration, its existence as an entity distinct from the thought is open to question."[68]

Thus, philosophers make use of the method of analysis to remove the obscurity of their own philosophical problems and to clarify their own thinking. And in this way the practice of analysis becomes different for different philosophers.

IV

According to Ayer, "The philosopher is not in a position to furnish speculative truths, which would, as it were, complete with the hypothesis of science, nor yet to pass a-priori judgements upon the validity of scientific theories, but that his function is to clarify the propositions of science by exhibiting their logical relationships, and by defining the symbols which occur in them."[69] In the movement of logical empiricism analysis appears in the form of logical analysis of language. The aims of logical analysis are: elimination of metaphysics and the clarification of conceptual confusions. To fulfil these aims philosophers provide definitions. But it does not follow from this that they compile a dictionary. For the definitions which philosophers provide are different from those which we find in dictionary.

Ayer makes a clear distinction between dictionary definitions and philosophical definitions. Dictionary definitions are, as he called them, explicit definitions; and the definitions which philosophy is required to provide are definition in use. In explicit definition when we define a symbol we put forward another symbol, or symbolic expression which is synonymous with it. The mass definitions which are given by us in every day life are of the examples of explicit definitions. Such as, 'Contagious is a communicating disease by contact,' or 'equanimity is an evenness of mind' or 'misanthropist is a hater of mankind.' Philosophy does not concern itself with these explicit definitions, but definitions in use. A symbol 'in use' is defined by showing how the sentences in which it significantly occurs can be translated into equivalent sentences, which contain neither the definiendum itself, nor any of its synonymus. For example a sentence "The round square cannot exist" is equivalent to "No one thing can be both square and round," and the sentence "The author of Waverley was Scotch" is equivalent to "One perons, and one person only, wrote Waverley, and that person was Scotch. By these typical examples Ayer makes it clear how 'definitions in use' is helpful to fulfil the aims of philosophy. The first of these examples provides us with a typical illustration of the way in which any definite descriptive phrase which occurs as the subject of a negative existential sentence can be eliminated; and the second, with a typical illustration of the way in which any definite descriptive phrase which occurs anywhere in any other type of sentence can be eliminated. Together, therefore, they show us how to express what is expressed by any sentence which contains a definite descriptive phrase without employing any such phrase. And thus they furnish us with a definition of these phrases in use.[70]

Philosophical analysis has no use of explicit definitions because it cannot serve the purpose of philosophical definition. The purpose of philosophical definition is to dispel those confusions which arise from our imperfect understanding of certain types of sentences in our language, where the need cannot be met by the provision of a synonym for any symbol, either because there is no synonym, or else because the available synonyms are unclear in the same fashion as the symbol to which the confusion is due. Ayer claims that A complete philosophical elucidation of any language would consist, first, in enumerating the types of sentence that were significant in that language, and then in displaying the relations of equivalence that held between sentences of various types. He explains that two sentences are said to be of the same type when they can be correlated in such a way that to each symbol in one sentence there corresponds a symbol of the same type in the other; and that two symbols are said to be of the same type when it is always possible to substitute one for the other without changing a significant sentence into a piece of nonsense.[71]

Thus for the philosophical analysis of any language one

should know the structure of that language. A factor which complicates the structure of a language such as English is the prevalence of ambiguous symbol.[72]

To say a symbol to be ambiguous is that the signs by which it is constituted are indentical not in their sensible form with one another but also with signs which are elements of not such symbol but of other symbol. For it is not merely an identity of form but also an identity of usage which makes two signs elements of the same symbol. Ayer takes the case of the sign "is". He says that if we were guided merely by the form of the sign, we should assume that the 'is' which occurs in the sentence. "He is the author of that book" was the same symbol as the "is" which occurs in the sentence "A cat is a mammal". But, when we come to translate the sentences, we find that the first is equivalent to "He, and no one else, wrote that books," and the second to "The class of mammals contains the class of cats." And this shows that in this instance, each "is" an ambiguous symbol which must not be confused with the other, nor with the ambiguous symbols of existence and class membership, and identity, and entailment, which also constituted by signs of the form "is". In Ayer's opinion a symbol is constituted by signs which are identical with one another in their sensible form, and in their significance, and a sign is a sense-content, or a series of sense-contents, which is used to convey literal meaning. But it does not infer from this view that a symbol is a collection of sense-contents. Ayer says that when we speak of certain objects, b, c, d..... as being elements of an object e, and of e as being constituted by b,c,d, ... we are not saying that they form part of e, in the sense in which my arm is a part of my body, —— What we are saying is that all the sentences in which symbol a occurs can be translated into sentences which do not contain a itself, or any symbol which is synonymous with e, but do contain symbols b,c,d, ... In such a case we say that e is a logical construction out of b,c,d.... there is a familiar example of table, the sentence I am now sitting in front of a table" can be translated into a sentence which does not mention tables, but only sense contents.... To say that tables are logical constructions out of sense-contents is to say not that the symbol "table" can be explicitly defined in terms of symbols which stand for sense-contents, but only that it can be so defined in use.[76] For definition in use does not provide a synonym for any symbol but its function is to enable us to translate sentences of a certain type.

Purpose

Ayer rejects the view, as it is said sometimes that the purpose of such philosophical definitions is to reveal the meaning of certain symbols, or combination of symbols. He objects that "it does not give an unequivocal description of the philosopher's practice, because it employs, in "meaning" a highly ambiguous symbol.[77] Because of this reason Ayer defines the relation of equivalence between sentences, without referring to the sign "meaning". He says, "if we are to use the sign "meaning" in the way in which it is most commonly used, we must not say that two sentences have the same meaning for any one, unless the occurence of one always has the same effect on his thoughts and actions as the occurance of the other.[78] But he says, "it is possible for two sentences to be equivalent, by our criterion, without having the same effect on anyone who employs the language. For instance, "P is a law of nature" is equivalent to "P is a general hypothesis which can always be relied on" : but the association of the symbol "law" are such that the former sentence tends to produce a very different psychological effect from its equivalent."[79] Philosophy is not concerned with the meaning of symbols. Because of its ambiguity" "meaning" leads the undiscarning critic to judge the result of a philosophical enquiry by a criterion which is not applicable to it, but only to an empirical enquiry concerning the psychological effect which the occurence of certain symbols has on a certain group of people."[80] Such empirical enquiries are quite distinct from the logical enquiries which constitute philosophy. According to Ayer they are an important element of sociology or of the scientific study of a language.

Ayer also rejects the view that philosophy tells us how certain symbols are used. "For", he argues "this suggests that the propositions of philosophy are factual propositions concerning the behaviour of a certain group of people; and this is not the case."[81] For example, "The philosopher who asserts that, in the English language, the sentence 'The author of Waverley was Scotch' is equivalent to "one person, and one person only, wrote Waverley, and that person was Scotch" is not asserting that all, or most, English speaking people use these sentences interchangeably. What he is asserting is that, in virtue of certain rules of entailment, namely those which are characteristic of "correct" English, every sentence which is entailed by "The author of Waverley was Sctoch," in conjunction with any given group of sentences, is entailed also by that group, in conjunction with "One person, and one person only, wrote Waverley, and that person was Scotch."[82] Thus he asserts, that "English speaking people should employ the verbal conventions that they do is, indeed, an empirical fact. But the deduction of relations of equivalence from the rules of entailment which characterise the English, or any other language is a purely logical activity; and it is in the logical activity, and not in any empirical study of the linguistic habits of any group of people, that analysis consists."[83] Thus in logical positivism, philosophical analysis is developed in the form of logical analysis of language. He further tells that "in most cases, the definitions are obtained from conventions which do, in fact, correspond to the utility of the definitions, as a means of clarification, that this should be so."[84] But the existence of such a correspondence is never part of what the definitions actually assert. He provides an example "if I wish to refute a philosophical opponent I do not argue about people's linguistic habits. I try to prove that his definitions involve a contradiction. Suppose, for example, that he is maintaining that "A is a free agent" is equivalent to 'A's actions are uncaused." Then I refute him by getting him to admit that "A is a free agent" is entitled by "A is morally responsible for his actions" whereas "A's actions are uncaused" entails A is not morally responsible for his actions.[85] Thus he refutes his definitions on the basis that they involve contradiction. "A is morally responsible for his actions" is nothing but a contradiction.

Ayer remarks that "the process of analysing a language is facilitated if it is possible to use for the classification of its forms an artificial system of symbols whose structure is known."[86] Russell and Whitehead employed the best known example of such a symbolism the so called system of logistic - in their famous work Principia Mathematica. But the language in which analysis is carried out should not be necessarily different from the language analysed. Ayer differs from Russell when he suggested, "that every language has a structure concerning which, in the language, nothing can be said, but that there may be another language dealing with the structure of the first language, and having itself a new structure, and that to this hierarchy of language there may be no limit."[87] Ayer does not agree with Russell. "This was written presumably in the belief that an attempt to refer to the structure of a language in the language itself would led to the occurence of logical peradoxes."[88] But Ayer agrees with Carnap who by "actually carrying out such an analysis, has subsequently shown that language can without self-contradiction be used in the analysis of itself."[89] Ayer clearly says, "The view of philosophy which we have adopted may fairly be described as a form of empiricism.... it is characteristic of an empiricist to eschew metaphysics on the ground that every factual proposition must refer to sense-experience. And even if the conception of philosophyzing as an activity of analysis is not to be discovered in the traditional theories of empiricists, we have seen that it is implicit in their practice."[90]

Thus in the logical empiricist movement philosophical analysis is shown in the form of logical analysis of language. By the logical analysis, they clarify the conceptual confusions and in doing so, they also eliminate the metaphysical propositions, because they are only due to conceptual confusions.

V

Logical analysis has influenced contemporary philosophical thought to a large extent. Gilbert Ryle, John

Wisdom, W.V.O. Quine, John Austin are the examples of this influence. The influence of Positivism, however, did not come to an end with the demise of the Circle. The ideas articulated by the original Positivists became topics of discussion throughout the world. By insisting that all metaphysics is nonsense, Positivism posed a serious threat to established religion, since most religion includes theology, and theology was considered a kind of metaphysics. Ammerman observes that in the United States, where Positivism almost from its inception had found many sympathetic listeners, the original doctrines of the circle have often been combined with the tradition of American Pragmatism. Since Pragmatism and Positivism have always shared many features, it is not surprising that some philosophers have been able to write in both traditions simultaneously. W.V.O. Quine is an excellent example of an original thinker who shows in his writings the influence of both Positivism and Pragmatism upon his thought.[91]

Gilbert Ryle and John Wisdom are two other important philosophers who are greatly influenced by Logical analysis. Although they differ in many respects from one another or from Logical empiricists but they shared a common interest in the analysis, as each of them understood the word, of ordinary forms of speech. The major work of Ryle, 'The Concept of Mind', clearly shows the influence of logical analysis. He attempts to show that the mental physical dichotomy which has dominated much metaphysical speculation since Descartes, is the result of a basic confusion about our use of mentalistic terms. This books and the various articles which Ryle wrote exploring other problems in similar ways have been enormously influencial in spreading interest in the methods of linguistic Analysis.

John Wisdom, who was a student of Wittgenstein, has given to logical analysis an original and exciting new kind of philosophical procedure. Unwillingly to reject metaphysics as merely nonsense, he attempts to understand why the metaphysician feels compelled to talk in their linguistically odd ways. By putting stress upon the imperfect similarities between various kinds of statements in our language, he hopes to discover what is and is not valuable in the various attempts to solve metaphysical questions. Many philosophers do not accept Wittgenstein's view that beyond dissolution of linguistic confusions there is no proper role for the philosopher. Linguistic confusions, of course, according to Wittgenstein, are due to misunderstanding of the logic of our language. "One of the most discussed of the younger analysts, P.F. Strawson", Ammerman writes, "has argued that there is no real antithesis between linguistic analysis and a certain kind of metaphysics. He distinguishes two kinds of metaphysics: that which only attempts to describe the conceptual boundaries of our language (descriptive metaphysics) and that which attempts to revise them (revisionary metaphysics). In his book 'Individuals' which he subtitled "An Essay in Descriptive Metaphysics." Strawson attempts to show, among other things, that certain general conclusions about the world can be gained from an analysis of how we speak. Presumably, this is the very thing that Wittgenstein was saying could not be done."[92]

Another important philosopher John Austin was also greatly influenced by logical analysis. He also believed that a great deal of what philosophers have written is not so much false as it is misleading and confused. However, Austin's procedure for dispelling this confusion is unique. Austin believed in the analysis of ordinary usages. Whose function is to analyse the language which is spoken by ordinary people. Ammerman writes, "Austin made few general pronouncements about the import of implications of his grammatical investigations. He does at times speak for the need of "a science of language," implying that such a science will supersede a great deal of what is now done by analytic philosophers. It seems to have been Austin's belief that the time is not yet ripe for speculation in philosophy. We must first become as clear as possible about how our knowledge operates before we attempt to settle philosophical problems or even speculate on whether any of them can be solved."[93] He says that "in spite of general similarity to Wittgenstein, Austin never endorsed Wittgenstein's speculations about the ultimate fate of philosophy."

Thus logical analysis has given a useful and worthy programme for philosophy. Although the practice is not something new for philosophy. All the great philosophers in the history of philosophy were interested in genuine philosophical analysis. But it is true that Ayer as an advocate of logical empiricism gives a new direction to analysis in the philosophy. Unlike other analysts. Ayer made a systematic application of the method of analysis to all the basic problems of philosophy and his approach, in doing so, has been thoughout an example of balance attitude of analysis.

Analysis is, of course, a valuable tool for removing certain barriers in the way of clear philosophical thinking and I agree with Ayer that analysis increases "our understanding of certain sentences and this is a benefit which the author of such a definition confers not only an others but also on himself."[94] But when Ayer claims that philosophy is linguistic analysis; it is not a doctrine but an activity, i.e., the activity of philosophizing, and the activity of philosophizing is analysis, I don't agree with him. For if it is so, the question arises, can analysis be regarded as an end itself? If analysis of propositions is an end in itself, then philosophy is reduced to either linguistics or logic. But it is different from them, and is also more than them. Philosophical is primarily an investigation into truth and values, and both of them are the standards on the basis of which propositions can be declared to be true or false. Analysis ignores the concrete realities of human situations for which all philosophy is intended. A man can not remain completely satisfied only with analysis in isolation from the values of life in the light of which an individual tries to realise the potentiality of his personality and seeks truth, beauty, happiness, justice etc., as the highest human values. Philosophy, therefore, is more concerned with reality and values. By reducing philosophy to analysis we make its field too narrow. And it is not much to say that the thesis of logical empiricism is a major attempt at philosophical suicide. All the great philosophers of the world devoted themselves to an investigation of the basic principles of knowledge and reality.

Does it mean that all such investigations which inspired and guided mankind for thousands of years are simply non-sense? C.E.M. Joad in his *Critique of Logical Positivism* admits that "philosophy has had the dual purpose of revealing truth and increasing virtue..... if Logical Positivism is right, philosophy cannot perform this function. It cannot help us to understand the universe, it cannot provide us with a synoptic view of the whole whose different departments are explored by the sciences and it cannot light up the dark places of the world. For there is no universe other than the different departments of natural fact explored by the sciences and the world contains no dark places at least, if certain matters are still obscure, that is only because science has not yet pushed its research for enough."[95]

Kalidas Bhattacharya in his *Philosophy, Logic and Language* writes, a "... language is secondary. If philosophy is granted only this secondary task of expressing what is known not only would this be undignified for philosophy, really there would be no task left for it, because every science and concrete discipline is under an equal obligation to express its points precisely. If certain expressions are clumsy or misleading, or if they give rise to puzzles and contradictions, it is for the respective science to be on their guard against them and correct them. Philosophy can do nothing here, because precision is to be effected by reference to the reals accepted as data, or established, by those sciences themselves."[96]

REFERENCES

1. J.O. Urmson, *Philosophical Analysis*, p. 116.
2. A.J. Ayer, *Language, Truth and Logic*, p. 52.
3. Ayer, *Revolution in Philosophy*, p. 98.
4. A.J. Ayer, *The Problem of Knowledge*, p. 7.
5. A.J. Ayer, *The Problem of Knowledge*, p. 7.
6. A.J. Ayer, *The Problem of Knowledge*, p. 9.
7. Ammerman, *Classics of Analytic Philosophy*, p. 2.

8. Wittgenstein, *Tractatus-Logico-Philosophicus*, p. 4. 112.
9. Hume, *An Enquiry concerning Human Understanding*. Sec. XII, Part III.
10. *The Central Questions of Philosophy*, p. 23.
11. Ayer, *Logical Positivism*, p. 13.
12. Epistle to the Reader in his *Essay Concerning Human Understanding*.
13. Ayer, *Language, Truth and Logic*, p. 83.
14. Ayer, *Language, Truth and Logic*, pp. 53-54.
15. Hume, *A Treatise of Human Nature*, Part III, Sec. XIV, pp. 165-66.
16. Ammerman, *Classics of Analytic Philosophy*, p. 3.
17. A.J. Ayer, *The Central Questions of Philosophy*, p. 34. J.O. Vrmson, *Philosophical Analysis*, p. 4.
18. *The Philoscphy of G.E. Moore*, Edited by P.A. Schilpp, p. 66.
19. Moore, *Philosophical Studies*, p. 289.
20. Ayer, *Central Questions of Philosophy*, p. 40.
21. Ayer, *Central Questions of Philosophy*, pp. 41-43.
22. "Analysis and the Unity of Russell's Philosophy" in *The Philosophy of Bernard Russel* ed. by P.A. Schilpp, p. 57.
23. Ayer, Russell, p. 58.
24. G.E. Moore, Is Existence a Predicate? Supplementary *Proceedings of the Aristotelion Society* XV (1936).
25. Ayer, *Russell*, p. 59.
26. Ayer, *Language Truth and Logic*, p. 23.
27. Ammerman, *Classics of Analytic Philosophy*, p. 6.
28. Wittgenstein, *Tractatus*, 4.003.
29. Wittgenstein, *Tractatus*, 4.461.
30. *Ibid.*, 4.2.

31. *Ibid.*, 4.464.
32. Article appeared in Ayer's *Revolution in Philosophy*.
33. Wittgenstein, *Philosophical Investigation*, Para 109, p. 47.
34. Ayer, *Central Questions of Philosophy*, p. 44.
35. Ayer, *Central Questions of Philosophy*, p. 44.
36. *Ibid.*, p. 44.
37. F.P. Ramsey, *The Foundations of Matahematics*, p. 263.
38. Ayer, *Central Questions of Philosophy*, p. 44.
39. Ayer, *Central Questions of Philosophy*, pp. 44-45.
40. *Ibid.*, p. 45.
41. *Ibid.*, p. 45.
42. *Ibid.*, p. 46.
43. Ayer, *Central Questions of Philosophy*, p. 46.
44. *Ibid.*, p. 46.
45. Ayer, *Central Questions of Philosophy*, p. 47.
46. *Ibid.*, pp. 47-48.
47. *Ibid.*, p. 48.
48. Ayer, *Central Questions of Philosophy*, p. 48.
49. *Ibid.*, p. 49.
50. *Ibid.*, pp. 49-50.
51. Ayer, *Central Questions of Philosophy*, p. 50.
52. *Ibid.*, p. 50.
53. *Ibid.*, p. 50.
54. *Ibid.*, p. 50.
55. L. Wittgenstein, *Philosophical Investigation*, para 43, p. 20.
56. *Ibid.*, Para 98, p. 45.
57. *Ibid.*, Para 124, p. 49.

58. Ayer, *Central Questions of Philosophy*, p. 52.
59. *Ibid.*, p. 52.
60. Wittgenstein, Para 109, p. 47.
61. Ayer, *Central Questions of Philosophy*, p. 53.
62. *Ibid.*, p. 56.
63. Ayer, *The Central Questions of Philosophy*, p. 58.
64. *Ibid.*, p. 58.
65. *The Central Questions of Philosophy*, p. 58.
66. *Ibid.*, p. 58.
67. *Ibid.*, p. 59.
68. *The Central Questions of Philosophy*, p. 59.
69. Ayer, *Language, Truth and Logic*, pp. 31-32.
70. Ayer, *Language, Truth and Logic*, p. 61.
71. Ayer, *Language, Truth and Logic*, p. 62.
72. *Ibid.*, p. 62.
73. Ayer, *Language, Truth and Logic*, p. 63.
74. *Ibid.*, p. 63.
75. *Ibid.*, p. 63.
76. Ayer, *Language, Truth and Logic*, p. 64.
77. *Ibid.*, p. 68.
78. *Ibid.*, p. 69.
79. Ayer, *Language, Truth and Logic*, p. 69.
80. *Ibid.*, p. 69.
81. *Ibid.*, pp. 69-70.
82. Ayer, *Language, Truth and Logic*, p. 70.
83. *Ibid.*, p. 70.
84. *Ibid.*, p. 70.

85. Ayer, *Language, Truth and Logic*, p. 70.
86. *Ibid.*, pp. 70-71.
87. Introduction to L. Wittgenstein's Tractus Logico-Philosophicus, p. 23.
88. Ayer, *Language, Truth and Logic*, p. 71.
89. *Ibid.*, p. 71.
90. *Ibid.*, p. 71.
91. Ammerman, *Classics of Analytic Philosophy*, pp. 8-9.
92. Ammerman, *Classics of Analytic Philosophy*, pp. 11-12.
93. *Classics of Analytic Philosophy*, p. 12.
94. Ayer, *Language, Truth and Logic*, p. 61.
95. C.E.M. Joad, *Critique of Logical Positivism*, pp. 29-30.
96. Bhattacharya, Kalidas, *Philosophy, Logic and Language*, pp. 11-12.

3

The Arguments Against the Possibility of Metaphysics

I

There are alternative periods of construction and destruction in the whole history of philosophy. One constructs a thesis, another destroys it; one give arguments in favour of that and another gives arguments against the thesis. Metaphysics is one of the important branches of philosophy which has been subjected to such a process of construction and destruction. Although arguments against the possibility of metaphysics are nothing new, but contemporary empiricism, which is also called logical empiricism, is characterized by D.M. Dutta as "the peak of the destructive movement."[1]

Although logical empiricists differ from one another in certain aspects of their views, but according to Ayer, "One thing which those of us who are called logical positivists tend to have in common is that we deny the possibility of philosophy as a speculative discipline."[2] Thus the main aims of Logical empiricism are — "first to provide a secure foundation for the sciences; and second to demonstrate the meaninglessness of all metaphysics,"[3] to full their second aim, i.e. to demonstrate the meaningless of metaphysics, they give arguments against the possibility of metaphysics.

But before examining their arguments we should know 'What is metaphysics'? 'What are the questions with which metaphysics deals'? According to the Encyclopedia the word "metaphysics" is drived from the Greek meta ta physika (literally, "after the things of nature"), an expression used by Hellenistic and later commentators to refer to Aristotle's untitled group of texts that we still call the metaphysics. Aristotle himself called the subjects of these texts First Philosophy, theology and sometimes wisdom, the phrase ta meta ta physica biblia ("the books after the books on nature") is not used by Aristotle himself and was apparently introduced by the editors who classified and catelogued his works."[4] It is said that "each of the special sciences deals only with a fragment of reality. Metaphysics goes beyond them in being concerned with reality as a whole."[5]

Another view about metaphysics is that the sciences deal with appearances, the metaphysician penetrates to the underlying reality. According to Ayer, "the reality is veiled from us, the discovery that things are not always what they seem appears to be incompatible with it. What possible experience could authorise our making a distinction between appearances as a whole and a quite different reality?"[6] The answer of metaphysicians would be that it is mystical experience. A metaphysician has a special faculty which unables him to see that reality is spiritual, or that time and space are not ultimately real, or that every thing is one. Questioning the validity of such experiences, Ayer writes, "If what they are said to establish does not make sense or, on any literal interpretation, is obviously false, then at the very least the case for their being cognitive has not been made out."[7] The logical empiricists attempt to extent the range of science over the whole area of systematic truth and for this they destroy the claims of idealist philosophers according to which there is a special kind of superscientific access to truth.

II

Though metaphysics has been criticized by its opponents since the Greek period, but such criticisms are of different kinds. Some believed that since metaphysics contradicts our empirical knowledge therefore it is false. Other anti-metaphysicians declared that the problems of metaphysics transcend the limit of human knowledge, therefore it is not certain. For Kant "Metaphysics is a completely isolated speculative science of reason, which soars for above the teachings of experience. .... It has not yet had the good fortune to enter upon the secure path of a science."[8] But he believed so on different grounds. According to him, "we can never transcend the limits of possible experience, though there is precisely what this science is concerned, above all else, to achieve. This situation yields, however, just the very experiment by which, indirectly, we are unable to prove the truth of this first estimate of an a-priori knowledge of reason, namely, that such knowledge has to do only with appearance and must leave the thing in itself as indeed real per se, but as not known by us. For what necessarily forces us to transcend the limits of experience and of all appearances is the unconditioned, by necessity and by right, demands in things in themselves, as required to complete the series of conditions."[9]

According to Ayer Kant made the impossibility of a transcendent metaphysics not as a matter of logic, but a matter of fact. Ayer makes a clear distinction between the approaches of Kant and logical empiricism. In Kant's view there is a transcendent reality, but the construction of our speculative reason is such that we can not hope to gain knowledge of it. Whereas on logical empiricists view to say that there is not a transcendent reality is to utter a pseudo proposition, a word series empty of logical content: and no supposition about the knowledge of a higher reality possesses by a higher being is for us even a significant hypothesis. The difference between the two views is best expressed by saying that while the speculative reason was in virtue of its own nature in capable of solving, our aim is to show that there are not genuine problems."[10]

Ayer's philosophy is best described as a form of empiricism. But in calling themselves empiricists, writes Ayer, "we are not avowing a belief in any of the psychological doctrines which are commonly associated with empiricism."[11]

The doctrine of Logical empiricism is different from traditional empiricism of Hume. Hume's empiricism is psychological, whereas the empiricism of logical positivism is logical. Hume held that impressions are the only objects of human mind, and therefore, if a word has meaning it must refer to an impression. In his 'Enquiries' Hume writes, "all the materials are derived either from our outward of inward sentiment: the mixture and composition of these belong alone to the mind and will. Or, to express myself in philosophical language, all our ideas or more feeble perceptions are copies of our impressions or more lively ones."[12] Hume's empiricism, further, differs from logical empiricists in that he affirmed the existence of trans-empirical world on the ground of faith. In his own words, "its best and most solid foundation is faith and divine revelation."[13]

Logical empiricists, on the other hand, do not hold any such belief. The arguments of logical empiricists against the possibility of metaphysics is that, its assertions were meaningless, since there was no possible way of verifying them in experience." Ayer writes Nothing that we could possibly experience, they argued, would serve to verify such assertions as 'the absolute is beyond time.' Therefore the positivists held, it tells us nothing."[14] The distinction between the attitude of earlier and later philosophers against the possibility of metaphysics is succinctly put up in the following statement: "....... whereas the earlier critics of metaphysics had generally been content to describe it as empty or useless of unscientific, the logical positivists took over from Wittgenstein Tractatus the rejection of metaphysics as meaningless. The proposition of metaphysics, they argued are neither true nor false, they are wholly devoid of significance."[15]

III

Following the early theory of Wittgenstein logical empiricists adopt the principle of verification to test whether a sentence is literally meaningful. A sentence is literally meaningful if it is either a tautology or empirically verifiable. Ayer also divides all genuine propositions into propositions which are concerned with "relation of ideas", and propositions which are concerned with "matters of fact." He writes, "The former class comprises the a-priori knowledge of logic and pure mathematics, and these I allow to be necessary and certain only because they are analaytic."[16]

A priori or analytic propositions "owe this certainly to the fact that they are tautologies." As Ayer remarks that when they say that analytic propositions are devoid of factual content, and consequently that they say nothing they are not suggesting that these propositions are senseless in the way that metaphysical utterances are senseless. For although they give us no information about any empirical situation, they do enlighten us by illustrating the way in which we use certain symbols. Thus if I say 'Nothing can be coloured in different ways at the same time with respect to the same part of itself,' I am not saying anything about the properties of any actual thing; but I am not talking nonsense. I am expressing an analytic proposition, which records our determination to call a colour expense which differs in quality from a neighbouring colour expense a different part of a given thing. In other words, I am simply calling attention to the implications of a certain linguistic usages."[17] Thus Ayer concludes "To say that a proposition is true a-priori is to say that it is a tautology. And tautologies though they may serve to guide us in our empirical search for knowledge, do not in themselves contain any information about any matter of fact."[18]

The criteria by which logical empiricists determine the validity of an empirical proposition is not the same as the criteria of an a-priori on an analytic proposition. For the validity of an a-priori proposition is purely formal whereas an empirical proposition is not. According to Ayer, an empirical proposition, or a system of empirical propositions, may be free from contradiction, and still be false. For example, "My newspaper contains news," is an analytic proposition, and "Newspaper is on the table in front of me" is an empirical proposition. It is self-contradictory to assert that my newspaper does not contain news, but it is not self-contradictory to assert that my newspaper is not on the table in front of me, although it happens to be false."[19] It is said to be false, not because it is formally defective, but because it fails to satisfy some material criterion."[20]

Truth and falsity of empirical propositions are judged by empirical criterion. For him, "We test the validity of an empirical hypothesis by seeing whether it actually fulfils the function which it is designed to fulfil.... The function of an empirical hypothesis is to enable us to anticipate experience. Accordingly, if an observation to which a given proposition is relevant confirms to our expectations, the truth of that proposition is confirmed. If the observation is contrary to our expectations, then the status of the proposition is jeoparised. We may preserve it by adopting or abandoning other hypothesis: or we may consider it to have been confuted."[21]

But even if an observation is relevant, one can not say that "the proposition has been proved absolutely valid, because it is still possible that a future observation will discredit it. But one can say that its probability has been increased."[22] And if an observation is contrary, "one can not say that it has been invalidated absolutely. For it is still possible that future observations will lead us to reinstate it. One can say only that its probability has been diminished.[25] Propositions which do not come in either category the category of analytic propositions and the category of empirical hypothesis are neither true nor false but meaningless.

The validity of an empirical proposition is tested by verification. Ayer thus formulates the principle of verification "A sentence had literal meaning if and only if the proposition it expressed was either analytic or empirically verifiable."[24] The principle of verification is concerned mainly with the empirical statements. Analytic judgements are mere tautologies, they give no information about the fact. Thus the criterion of verifiability is the criterion to test the genuineness of apparent statements of fact. Ayer says, "a sentence is factually significant to any given person, if, and only if, he knows how to verify the proposition which it purports to express that is, if he knows what observation would lead him, under certain conditions, to accept the proposition as being true or reject it as being false."[25]

The customary answer to the question 'What is it that determines the truth or falsehood of empirical proposition as Ayer says in his paper entitled Verification and Experience, is, in effect, that it is their agreement on disagreement with reality." He says "in effect" because he wishes to allow alternative formulation. He writes, "There are some who could speak of correspondence or accordance rather than agreement; some who for the word "reality" would substitute "facts" or "experience".[26] But according to Ayer the choice of different words does not reflect any important difference of meaning. Though Ayer himself believes this answer to be true, but in his view it requires some elucidation. For the sake of simplification he draws a distinction between those empirical propositions whose truth or falsehood cannot be directly determined but they can be determined only by ascertaining the truth or falsehood of other propositions and those whose truth and falsehood can be determined directly by observation.

Universal propositions are of the former class whose truth or false hood cannot be directly established. For example, "We cannot directly establish the truth or falsehood of the proposition that gold as dissoluble in aqua regia, unless of course we regard this as a definite attribute of gold and so make the proposition into a tautology. We test it by establishing the truth or falsehood of singular propositions relating, among other things, to particular pieces of gold. We may indeed deduce one universal proposition from another, or even infer it by analogy. "But" he clearly states, in all such cases we must finally arrive at a proposition for which the evidence consists solely in the truth or falsehood of certain singular propositions.[27]

Here Ayer remarks that in establishing this they are never entitled to regard the universal proposition as conclusively verifiable. He says, "However often we may have observed the dissolution of pieces of gold in aqua regia, we must still allow it to be possible that the next piece with which we experiment will not so dissolve. On the other hand, the falsity of any one of the relevant singular propositions does entail the falsity of the universal proposition."[28] There is a logical assymetry in the relationship of universal and singular propositions.

Thus, to test the validity of an universal proposition such as 'gold is dissoluble in aqua regia' is to ascertain the truth or falsehood of singular propositions which refer to particular pieces of gold. But these propositions, in their turn, depend for their verification upon the verification of other propositions. By taking a similar example, he says, "For a piece of gold is a material thing; and to test the validity of propositions referring to material thing, we must ascertain the truth or falsehood of propositions referring to sense data."[29] Here Ayer says that he had another instance of logical assymetry. For a proposition referring to a material thing may entail proposition referring to sense-data, but a proposition referring to sense-data may not entail proposition referring to a material thing. Ayer proposes to call those proposition as basic propositions whose truth or falsehood can be determined directly by observation. He writes," If the distinction which we have drawn between them and other propositions is legitimate, we may confine ourselves to questions concerning the nature of basic propositions and the manner in which our determination of their validity depends upon our experience."[30]

Here he points out that for example Otto Neurath and Carl Hempel[31] maintain that to compare propositions with facts or reality or experience is nonsensical. They maintain that a proposition can be compared with another propositions. They believe in a class of propositions. According to Neurath, to express a protocol proposition, a sentence should contain name or description of an observer and some words referring to an act of observation. Ayer argues, "Neurath makes the truth and falsehood of any proposition whatsoever depend upon its compatibility or incompatibility with other propositions. He recognizes no other criterion. In this respect, his protocol propositions are not allowed any advantage. If we are presented with a protocol proposition and also with a non-protocol proposition and also with a non-protocol proposition which is incompatible with it we are not obliged to accept the protocol proposition and reject the other. We have an equal right to reject either. But if this is so we need not bother to devise a special form for protocol proposition in order to ensure their stability."[32]

Ayer wonders why Neurath and Hempal pay so much attention to protocol propositions, in as much as the distinction which they draw between protocol propositions and other propositions is merely a distinction of form. By a protocol proposition they do not mean that which is directly verified by observation, but they use the term purely as a syntactical designation for a certain assemblage of words. Similarly Carnap equivocates with this term.

According to Carnap[33] the question concerning the nature of protocol statement depend on conventions about forms of words. Ayer argues, "If the term" protocol statement" was being used merely as a syntactical designation for certain combinations of symbols then our choice of the sentences to which we applied it would indeed be a matter of convention. It would involve no more reference to truth than a decision to apply the designation "basic" to all English sentences beginning with B. But this is not the sense in which Carnap is supposed to be using the term. He is using it not mark out the form of certain statements, but rather to express the fact that they refer to what is immediately given. Accordingly, our answer to his question "What kinds of words occur in protocol statements"? cannot depend simply upon a conventional choice of linguistic forms. It must depend upon the way in which we answer the question "What objects are the elements of given, direct experience"? And this is not a matter of language, but a matter of fact."[34]

Thus, Ayer concludes, "the forms of basic propositions depend partly indeed upon linguistic conventions but partly also upon the nature of the given."[35] In this way Ayer proves that the philosophers who reject the notion of agreement with reality as a criterion of truth, the legitimacy of the distinction which is drawn between those empirical propositions whose truth or falsehood can be determined by ascertaining the truth or falsehood of other propositions and those whose truth or falsehood can be determined directly by observation, is implicitly acknowledge even by them.

Ayer differs in some respects even from those philosophers who accept the notion of agreement with reality as a criterion of truth. He says, "It is sometimes suggested that this relation of agreement is of the same kind as that of which it is a picture."[36] As Wittgenstein, in his Tractatus says "A proposition is a picture of reality."[37] Ayer does not think that this is true. His argument is, "If any propositions are picture, presumably false propositions are so as well as true ones. In other words, we cannot tell from the form of the proposition, that is, merely by looking at the picture, whether it depicts a real situation or not. But how then are we to distinguish the true picture agrees with reality whereas the false one does not? But in that case the introduction of the notion of picturing does not serve our purpose. It does not enable us to dispense with the notion of agreement."[38]

Further he says, "The same objections hold against those who say that this relation of agreement is one of identity of structure. This is to treat propositions as if they were maps. But then it is to be supposed that a false proposition is also a map. The mere form of the proposition will not tell us whether the country which it purports to map is imaginary or real."[39] Sometimes it is suggested that they ought in connection of proposition and facts to introduce the notion of causation. Ayer says, "The relation, it may be said, between the proposition" I am in pain" and the fact that verifies it is that the fact causes me to assert the proposition, or at any rate to believe it." But Ayer clearly asserts that verification cannot be analyzed in terms of it. In any case, he says "... my being in pain will verify the proposition that I am in pain, Why? Because when I say "I am in pain" I mean that I am in pain, and if P then P. But how do I establish P ? How do I know that I really am in pain? Again the answer can only be "I feel it."[2]

Ayer regards basic propositions as "incorrigible". Ayer asserts that "What is meant by their being incorrigible is that it is impossible to be mistaken about them except in a verbal sense. In a verbal sense, indeed, it is always possible to misdescribe one's experience; but if one intends to do no more than record what is experienced without relating it to anything else, it is not possible to be factually mistaken; and the reason for this is that one is making no claim that any further fact could confute."[41] In the principle of verification Ayer does not use the term verification in the sense in which basic propositions are verifiable. He clearly states, "If the principle of verification is to be seriously considered as a criterion of meaning, it must be interpreted in such a way as to admit statements that are not so strongly verifiable as basic statements are supposed to be."[42]

Then the question arises 'What is to be understood by the term "verifiable" in this context?' To make it clear, Ayer draws a distinction between practical verifiability and verifiability in principle or theoretical verifiability. According to him, "we all understand, in many cases believe, propositions which we have not in fact taken steps to verify. Many of these are propositions which we could verify if we took enough trouble. But there remain a number of significant propositions, concerning matters of fact, which we could not verify even if we chose: simple because we lack the practical means of placing ourselves in the situation where the relevant observations could be made."[43] So in many cases, he says, that "I am unable to decide the matter by actual observation. But I do know what observations would decide it for me, if, as is theoretically conceivable, I were once in a position to make them. And therefore, I say that the proposition is verifiable in principle, if not in practice, and is accordingly significant."[44]

He makes a further distinction between the "strong" and the "weak" sense of the term "verifiable". According to him, "A proposition is said to be varifiable in the strong sense of the term, if, and only if, its truth could be conclusively established in experience. But it is verifiable, in the weak sense, if it is possible for experience to render it probable."[45] Though other positivists like Moritz Schlick and Friedrich Weismann[46] proposed to adopt conclusive verifiabaility as the criterion of significance, in Ayer's view, it is not acceptable.

Ayer considers the case of general propositions of law such as, "arsenic is poisonous"; all men are mortal; a body tends to expand when it is heated. He writes, "It is of the very nature of these propositions that their truth cannot be established with certainty by any finite series of observations. But if it is recognised that such general propositions of law are designed to cover an infinite number of cases, then it must be admitted that they cannot, even in principle, be verified conclusively. And then if we adopt conclusive verifiability as our criterion of significance, we are logically obliged to treat these general propositions of law in the same fashion as we treat the statements of the metaphysician."[47]

To face this difficulty Schlick, in his Positivism and Realism points out that due to practical disability the proposition "there is a mountain 10,000 feet high on the other side of the moon," we are not and never be in a position to verify it. According to Ayer Schlick has adopted the heroic course of saying that these general propositions are pieces of nonsense, albeit an essentially important type of nonsense. But here the introduction of the term "important" is simply an attempt to hedge. It serves only to mark the author's recognition that their view is somewhat too paradoxical, without in any way removing the paradox. Besides, the difficulty is not confined to the case of general propositions of law, though it is there revealed most plainly. It is hardly less obvious in the case of propositions about the remote past. For it must surely be admitted that, however srong the evidence in favour of historical statements may be, their truth can never become more than highly probable. And to maintain that they also constituted an important, or unimportant, type of nonsense would be unplausible, to say the very least.[48] Thus Ayer asserts, the principle that a sentence can be factually significant only if it expresses what is conclusively verifiable is self-stultifying as a criterion of significance. For it leads to the conclusion that it is impossible to make a significant statement of fact at all.[49]

Nor does Ayer accept the suggestion which is proposed by Karl Popper[50] that a sentence should be allowed to be factually significant if, and only if, it expresses something which is definitely confutable by experience. According to Ayer this assumption is false. He argues, "A hypothesis cannot be conclusively confuted any more than it can be conclusively verified. For when we take the occurrences of certain observations as proof that a given hypothesis is false, we presuppose the existence of certain conditions. And though, in any given case, it may be extremely improbable that this assumption is false, it is not logically impossible." He asserts that "there need be no self-contradiction in holding that some of the relevant circumstances are other than we have taken them to be. And if it is not the case that any hypothesis can be definitely confuted, we cannot hold that the genuineness of a proposition depends on the possibility of its definite confulation."[51] Accordingly, Ayer falls back on the weaker sense of verification. When he speaks of the empirical verification, he means nothing more than the weaker sense of verification.

IV

Thus, Ayer demonstrates that any metaphysical question is nonsensical. His charge against the metaphysician is that "he produces sentences which fail to conform to the conditions under which alone a sentence can be literally significant."[52] Metaphysicians themselves cannot reject the view that their statements are not verifiable in this sense. For they neither regard them analytic, for otherwise they would be nothing more than tautologies, nor they regard them verifiable, for otherwise the truth on falsehood of these statements would depend upon experience.

As an illustration, in his Verification and Experience, Ayer takes the case of the man who claims to have an immediate non-sensory experience of God. He says, "So long as he uses the word "God" simply as a name for the content of his experience, I have no right to disbelieve him. Not having such experience myself I cannot understand him fully. I do not myself know what it is like to be acquainted with God. But I can at least understand that he is having some experience of a kind that I do not have. And this I may readily believe. At the same time it must be remarked that "God" in this usage cannot be the name of a transcendent being." "For" Ayer argues, to say that one was immediately acquainted with a transcendent being would be self-contradictory. And though it might be the name of a person who in fact endured forever one could not say that one was immediately acquainted with him as enduring for ever. For this, too, would be self contradictory. Neither would the fact that people were acquainted with God, in this sense, offer a valid ground for inferring that the world had a first cause, on that human beings survived death, or in short that anything existed which had the attributes that are popularly ascribed to God."[53]

Thus, clearly metaphysicians can not avoid making their statement non-verifiable. For if they avoid they can not serve their purpose. And if these statements are not verifiable in experience then logical empiricists cannot accept them as meaningful statements. They say that they are non-sensical.

According to Ayer, "The metaphysicians does not intend to write nonsense. He lapses into it through being deceived by grammar, or through committing errors of reasoning."[54] Rudolf Carnap in his article The Elimination of Metaphysics through Logical Analysis of Language,[55] asserts that the chief sources of meaningless statements are, first they "contain meaningless words." For example, "this thing is toovy." It is a meaningless. The word "toovy" has no existencial import. There is no such thing as "toovy". Secondly, "they consist of meaningful words, but the words are put together in such a way that nevertheless no meaning results." For example, he says, "Caesor is a prime number," here all words are meaningful, but they are not in accordance with the rules of syntax. "Prime number" cannot be affirmed of or denied to a person, since it is a predicate of numbers. "Caesor is a general" is a genuine statement. Thus, in the second type of meaningless statement "the word sequence is formed counter syntactically."

In this way he divides the meaningless statements into two forms: Counter-Semantical and Counter-Syntactical statements. These propositions are called "pseudo-propositions" by logical empiricists. Carnap says, "since it looks like a statement, yet is not a statement, does not assert anything, expresses neither a true nor a false proposition, we call this word sequence a "pseudo-statement". Similarly Ayer writes, "a Pseudo-proposition being a series of words that may seem to have the structure of a sentence but is in fact meaningless."[56]

Ayer assets that the prime source of metaphysics is linguistic confusions. A metaphysician is misled by a superficial grammatical feature, of his language. Ayer takes an instance of the way "in which a consideration of grammar leads to metaphysics is the case of the metaphysical concept of Being."[57] He says, "The origin of our temptation to raise questions about being, which no conceivable experience would enable us to answer, lies in the fact, in our language, sentences which express existential propositions and sentences which express attributive propositions may be of the same grammatical form. For instance, the sentences "Martyrs exist" and "Martyrs suffer" both consist of a noun followed by an intransitive verb, and the fact that they have grammatically the same appearance leads one to assume that they are of the same logical type. It is seen that in the proposition" Martyrs suffer," the members of a certain species are credited with a certain attribute, and it is sometimes assumed that the some thing is true of such a proposition as "Martyrs exist." If this were actually the case, it would, indeed, be as legitimate to speculate about the being of martyrs as it is to speculate about their suffering."[58]

But Ayer asserts as of Kant,[59] that existence is not an attribute. For Ayer argues, "when we ascribe an attribute to a thing, we covertly assert that it exists so that if existence were itself an attribute, it would follow that all positive existential propositions were tautologies, and all negative existential propositions self-contradictory; and this is not the case." So, Ayer affirms that those who raise questions about being which are based on the assumption that existence is an attribute are guilty of following grammar beyond the boundaries of sense.

He gives another example in which the same mistake has been made. The example is "Unicorns are fictitious." In this proposition there is a superficial grammatical resemblance between the English sentences "Dogs are faithful" and "Unicorns are fictitious," and between the corresponding sentences in other languages, creates the assumption that they are of the same logical type. Dogs must exist in order to have the property of being faithful, and so it is held that unless unicorns in some way existed they could not have the property of being fictitious. But as it is plainly self contradictory to say that fictitious objects exist, the device is adopted of saying that they are real in some non-empirical sense. But since there is no way of testing whether an object is real in this sense, as there is for testing whether it is real in the ordinary sense, the assertion that fictitious objects have a special non-empirical mode of real being is devoid of all literal significance. It comes to be made as a result of the assumption that being fictitious is an attribute. This fallacy is of the same order as that of supposing that existence is an attribute.

"The postulation of real non-existent entities, "Ayer says, "results from the superstition that to every word or phrase that can be the grammatical subject of a sentence, there must somewhere be a real entity corresponding. For as there is no place in the empirical world for many of these "entities" a special non-empirical world is invoked to house them."[61] According to Ayer, this error is not only attributed to the utterence of a Heidegger who bases his metaphysics on the assumption that "Nothing" is a name which is used to denote something peculiarly mysterious, but also the prevalence of such problems as those concerning the reality of propositions and universals whose senselessness, though less obvious, is no less complete. It is not necessary to take a list of metaphysical terms such as the Absolute, the Unconditioned, the Ego, and so forth, and prove each of them to be meaningless: For, as Ayer says in his article Demonstration of the Impossibility of Metaphysics, it follows from the task metaphysics sets itself that all its assertion must be non-sense. For it is the aim of metaphysics to describe a reality lying beyond experience, and therefore any proposition which would be verified by empirical observation is ipso facto not metaphysical. But what no observation could verify is not a proposition. The fundamental postulate of metaphysics "There is a super - (or hinter - phenomenal reality," is itself not a proposition. For there is no observation or series of observations we could conceivably make by which its truth or falsehood would be determined. It may seem to be a proposition, having the sensible form of a proposition. But nothing is asserted by it."[62]

Metaphysicians also construct the counter-syntactical propositions, such as, "things in-themselves" "Cogito Ergo Sum" (I think therefore I am), etc., in which the words are meaningful but they are not in accordance with the rules of syntex. Ayer examines the case of Descartes' 'Cogito Ergo Sum' which is the outcome of method of doubt. He doubts everything but the doubter. It is all due to deductive reasoning that he asserts the existence of the doubter. Ayer observes, that Descartes attempted to derive all human knowledge from premises whose truth was intuitively certain; but this interpretation puts an undue stress on the element of psychology in his system.

Ayer argues, "what he was really trying to do was to base all our knowledge on propositions which it would be self-contradictory to deny. He thought he had found such a proposition in "Cogito" which must not here understood in its ordinary sense of "I think" but rather as meaning "there is a thought now". In fact he was wrong, because, "non Cogito" would be self-contradictory only if it negated itself: and this no significant proposition can do. But even if it were true that such a proposition as "there is a thought now" was logically certain, it still would not serve Descates' purpose. For if "cogito" is taken in the sense, his initial principle "cogito ergo sum" is false. "I exist" does not follow from "there is a thought now."

Thought does not entail the thinker. Ayer says, "no one event intrinsically points to any other. We infer the existence of events which we are not actually observing, with the help of general principles. But these principles must be obtained inductively. By mere deduction from what is immediately given we cannot advance a single step beyond."[64] But the metaphysicians deduce an unobservable event from observing thing or from the general principle which are also obtained deductively. And this is their fault. Thus according to Ayer, "The only other course open to one who wished to deduce all our knowledge from "first principles," would be of take from his premises a set of a-priori truths." But he argues "an a-priori truth is a tautology. And from a set of tautologies, taken by themselves, only further tautologies can be validly deduced. But it would be absurd to put forward a system of tautologies as constituting the whole truth about the universe."[65] Thus, the assertion" Cogito ergo sum" is neither a-priori nor empirically verifiable and therefore it is a meaningless - "pseudo proposition."

Although metaphysicians themselves agree with the view that metaphysical statements cannot be verified in the empirical world, but when logical positivists say that they are not verifiable because they are without sense, then it is the point of dispute. Professor Carnap writes, "some-one may object: these statements is the metaphysical books obviously have an effect upon the reader, and sometimes a very strong effect, therefore they certainly express something. That is quite true, they do express something, but nevertheless they have no sense, no theoretical content. He gives an answer to the objection in his 'Philosophy and Logical Syntex' where he distinguishes two functions of languages (1) the expressive function and (2) the representative of cognitive function. In his view, almost all the conscious and unconscious movements of a person including the linguistic utterances, express something of his feelings, his present mood, his temporary or permanent dispositions to reactions, and the like. Therefore we may take almost all his movements and words as symptoms from which we can infer something about the feelings or his character. That is the expressive function of movements and words. But besides that a certain portion of linguistic utterances (e.g. "this book is black") as distinguished from other linguistic utterances and movements has a second function: these utterances represents a certain state of affairs; they tell us that something is the case; they assert something, they predict something, they judge something.[66]

He makes a further distinction between the assertion and the expression. He gives an example, "if somebody is laughing we may take this as a symptom of his merry mood; if on the other hand he tells us without laughing: 'Now I am merry,' we can learn from his words the same thing which we inferred in the first case from his laughing. Nevertheless, there is a fundamental difference between the laughter and the words; : 'I am merry now.' This linguistic utterance asserts the merry mood, and therefore it is either true or false. The laughter does not assert the merry mood but expresses it. It is neither true nor false, because it does not assert anything, although it may be either genuine or deceptive." Carnap says, "Many linguistic utterances are analogous to laughing in that they have only an expressive function, no representative function. Examples of this are cries like "Oh, Oh" or, on a higher level, lyrical verses." Thus the anti-metaphysical thesis of logical empiricists asserts "Metaphysical statements — like lyrical verses — have only an expressive function, but no representative function."[67]

After all there is a great differences between metaphysics and lyrics. Carnap affirms that metaphysician believes that in his metaphysical treatise he has asserted something, and that is led by this into argument and polemics against the statements of some other metaphysicians. Whereas a poet does not assert that the verses of another are wrong or erroneous; he usually contents himself with calling them bad. A logical empiricist does not criticise the non-theoretical character of any art. Carnap writes, "The non-theoretical character of metaphysics would not be in itself a defect, all arts have this non-theoretical character without losing their high values for personal as well as for social life." According to him "the danger lies in the deceptive character of metaphysics; it gives the illusion of knowledge without actually giving any knowledge. This is the reason why we reject it."[68] In Ayer's opinion the view that the metaphysician is to be reckoned among the poets appears to rest on the assumption that both talk nonsense. But this assumption is false. In the vast majority of cases the sentences which are produced by poets do have literal meaning. He says, "The difference between the man who uses language scientifically and the man who uses it emotively is not that the one produces sentences which are incapable of arousing emotion, and the other sentences which have no sense, but that the one is primarily concerned with the expression of true propositions, the other with the creation of a work of art. Thus, if a work of science contains true and important propositions, its value as a work of science will hardly be diminished by the fact that they are inelegantly expressed. And similarly, a work of art is not necessarily the worse for the fact that all the propositions comprising it are literally false."[69] But he clearly asserts, "to say that many literary works are largely composed of falsehood, is not to say that they are composed of pseudo-propositions. It is, in fact, very rare for a literary artist to produce sentences which have no literal meaning. And where this does occur, the sentences are carefully chosen for their rhythm and balance. If the author writes nonsense, it is because he considers it most suitable for bringing about the effects for which his writing is designed."[70] On the other hand, the metaphysician does not intend to write non-sense but "he lapses into it through being deceived by the grammar or through committing errors of reasoning."[71]

V

The technique of the logical analysis of language is not applied by the logical empiricists only to the propositions of metaphysics but also in respect of the propositions of ethics, aesthetics and religion, because all these branches of philosophy believes in the existence of super-natural entity in the same way as that of Metaphysics. Ayer says, "The Vienna Circle as a whole was not greatly interested in ethics." The only question with which logical empiricists were concerned was "whether ethical statements belonged within the fold, whether they were statements of fact at all."[72] According to M. Schlick "the emotive theory of ethics was characteristic of logical positivism."[73] The assertions of value do not express propositions, they merely express feeling. They are not "scientific" assertions but "emotive". And therefore there is no question of truth or falsehood with them.

Ayer devides all ethical propositions into four classes and proves that they are not propositions at all.[74] Only first type of propositions, "relating to the definitions of ethical terms," in his opinion, "can be said to constitute ethical philosophy." Other types of propositions "which describe the phenomena of moral experience, and their causes, must be assigned to the science of psychology, or sociology. The exhortation to moral virtue are not propositions at all, but ejaculations or commands which are designed to provoke the reader to action of a certain sort. Accordingly, they do not belong to any branch of philosophy or science." The fourth type of propositions "the expressions of ethical judgement" he says, "are neither definitions nor comments upon definitions, nor quotations, we may say decisively that they do not belong to ethical philosophy. "Therefore Ayer writes, "A strictly philosophical treatise on ethics should make no ethical pronouncements." Being a radical empiricist, Ayer is not concerned "whether "good" can be defined in terms of "right" or "right" in terms of "good" or both in terms of "value"." But, "whether statements of ethical value can be translated into statements of empirical facts."

Logical empiricists reject both the subjectivist view and utilitarian view of ethics. Subjectivists define morality in terms of the feelings of approval which a certain person, or group of people, has towards them. In this sense, to say "X is good" or "X is right" is to say X is approved of by myself or by a group of people. Ayer rejects this view because "it is not self contradictory to assert that some actions which generally approved of are not right or that some things which are generally approved of are not good."[75] Similarly he rejects the view that it is approved of by myself. In his own words, "we reject the alternative subjectivist view that a man who asserts that a certain action is right or that a certain thing is good, is saying that he himself approved of it, on the ground that a man who confessed that he sometimes approved of what was bad or wrong would not be contradicting himself."[76] Thus, Ayer rejects the subjectivist view by the method of logical analysis of language. As this method has proved that the judgement would be certain only if it contradicts itself. Such as "X is X" would be true if it contradicts "X is not X".

Further, he rejects the utilitarian view by the same argument. The utilitarians define morality "in terms of pleasure, or happiness or satisfaction, to which they give rise." Ayer is in opposition of this view. He gives the same argument that "since it is not self-contradictory to say that some pleasant things are not good, or that some bad things are desired, it can not be the case that the sentence "X is good" is equivalent to "X is pleasant" or to "X is desired."[77] Thus, Ayer proves that the proposition "relating to the definitions of ethical terms" do not express proposition at all. The ethical judgements are nothing but "people's feelings." "The validity of ethical judgements," he says, "is not empirically calculable."

In this connection, he makes a distinction between normative ethical symbols and descriptive ethical symbols. In saying, "X is wrong" if it constitutes a sentence which states that a certain type of conduct is repugnent to the moral sense of a particular society..., the symbol "wrong" is a descriptive ethical symbol, and the sentence in which it occurs expresses an ordinary sociological proposition." And if X is wrong constitutes "a sentence which expresses a moral judgement concerning a certain type of conduct— the symbol "wrong" is a normative ethical symbol, and the sentence in which it occurs does not express an empirical proposition at all."[78] And it is plain that "it is only with normative ethics that we are at present concerned."[79] But in saying that "the validity of ethical judgements — must be regarded as "absolute" or "intrinsic", or "normative ethical concepts," it does not follow that Ayer believes in the absolutist view of ethics, which holds that "statements of value are not controlled by observation, as ordinary empirical propositions are, but only by a mysterious "intellectual intuition."[80] Ayer opposes this view also, He argues, "For it is notorious that what seems intuitively certain to one person may seem doubtful, or even false, to another. So that unless it is possible to provide some criterion by which one may decide between conflicting intuitions, a mere appeal to intuition is worthless as a test of a proposition's validity."[81] He does agree with absolutists by admitting that the fundamental ethical concepts are unanalaysable. But whereas the absolutists say them unanalysable in the sense that they are controlled by a mysterious "intellectual intuition" and are intuitively certain; they can not be empirically analysed, Ayer calls them unanalysable in the sense that "they are mere pseudo-concepts." He says, The presence of an ethical symbol in a position adds nothing to its factual content."[82] In this sense "You acted wrongly in stealing that money" is equivalent to "You stole that money." He writes, "In adding that this action is wrong I am not making any further statement about it. I am simply evincing my moral disapproval of it. It is as if I had said "You stole that money" in a peculiar tone of horror, or written it with the addition of some special exclamation marks. The tone, or the exclamation marks, adds nothing to the literal meaning of the sentence. It merely serves to show that the expression of it is attended by certain feelings in the speaker."[83] He generalises this statement into ethical terms "Stealing money is wrong" and say "I produce a sentence which has no factual meaning — that is, expresses no proposition which can be either true or false." "Stealing money is wrong" is nothing more than "Stealing money."[84]

In this opinion the assertions of value are not scientific but emotive. According to him, "In saying that a certain type of action is right or wrong, I am not making any factual statement, nor even a statement about my own state of mind. I am merely expressing certain moral sentiments. And the man who is ostensibly contradicting me is merely expressing his moral sentiments. So that there is plainly no sense in asking which of us is in the right. For neither of us in asserting a genuine proposition."[85]

He maintains that ethical terms do not serve only to express feeling but they are also calculated to arouse feeling, and so to stimulate action. Some of the ethical terms are used as commands, for example, the sentence "It is your duty to tell the truth" or the sentence "You ought to tell the truth," is regarded both as the expression of a certain sort of ethical feeling about truthfulness and as the expression of the command "Tell the truth." The sentence "It is good to tell the truth" also involves the command more than a suggestion. Thus, Ayer says, the "meaning" of the word "good," in its ethical usage, is differentiated from that of the word "duty" or the word "ought". In fact we may define the meaning of the various ethical words in terms both of the different feelings they are ordinarily taken to express, and also the different responses which they are calculated to provoke."[86] Thus to say that to find a criterion for determining the validity of ethical judgements is impossible is not to say that they have an "absolute" validity which is not dependent on ordinary sense experience, but they have no objective validity. He says, "sentences which simply express moral judgements do not say anything. They are pure expressions of feeling and as such do not come under the category of truth and falsehood. They are unverifiable for the same reason as a cry of pain or a word of command is universifiable because they do not express genuine pro-prositions."[87]

In this opinion, "ethics, as a branch of knowledge is nothing more than a department of psychology and sociology."[88] In saying this he says that he is not over-looking the existence of casuistry. Ayer remarks that casuistry is not a science. According to him, "it is a purely analytical investigation of the structure of a given moral system. In other words it is an exercise in formal logic."[89] In this connection Ayer accounts for the ethical theories of Kant and Hedonism. Kant speaks of "categorical imperative". According to Ayer, "one of the chief causes of moral behaviour is fear, both conscious and unconscious, of a god's displeasure, and fear of the enmity of society. And this is the reason why moral percepts present themselves to some people as "categorical" command."[90] To account for the hedonistic theory of morals, Ayer says "one finds that the moral code of society is partly determined by the beliefs of that society concerning the conditions of his own happiness or in other words, that a society tends to encourage or discourage a given type of conduct by the use of moral sanctions according as it appears to promote or destruct from the contentment of the society as a whole. And this is the reason why altruism is recommended in most moral codes and egotism condemned."[91] According to Ayer, "each of these theories ignores the fact which lies at the root of the other, both may be criticized as being one sided; but this is not the main objection to either of them. Their essential defect is that they treat propositions which refer to the causes and attributes of our ethical feelings as if they were definitions of ethical concepts. And thus they fail to recognise that ethical concepts are pseudo-concepts and consequently indefiniable."[92]

Similarly for Ayer, his conclusion about the nature of ethics apply to aesthetics also. For he says, "Aesthetic terms are used in exactly the same way as ethical terms. Such aesthetic words as "beautiful" and "hideous" are employed, as ethical words are employed, not to make statements of fact, but simply to express certain feelings and evoke a certain response. It follows, as in ethics, that there is no sense in attributing objective validity to aesthetic judgements, and no possibility of arguing about questions of value in aesthetics, but only about questions of fact."[93] A scientific treatment of aesthetics, Ayer says, "Would show us what in general were the causes of aesthetic feeling, why various societies produced and admired the works of art they did, why taste varies as it does within a given society, and so forth."[94] These questions are psychological or sociological in their character. In Ayer's view, "They have little or nothing to do with aesthetic criticism as we understand it. But that is because the purpose of aesthetic criticism is not so much to give knowledge as to communicate emotion. The critic, by calling attention to certain features of the work under review, and expressing his own feelings about them, endeavours to make us share his attitude towards the work as a whole. The only relevant propositions that he formulates are propositions describing the nature of the work. And these are plain records of fact."[95]

The logical empiricists also reject the validity of religious propositions and give arguments against the possibly of transcendental god. For the mention of God brings them to the possibility of religious knowledge. Although by their treatment of metaphysics this possibility of religious knowledge has already been ruled out, but as they feel that this is a point of considerable interest they discuss it too. According to the logical empiricists "the existence of a being having the attributes which define the god of any non-animistic religion cannot be demonstratively proved."[96] For, if the conclusion that a god exists is to be demonstratively certain, then the premises must be certain. Because the conclusion of any deductive argument is already contained in its premises. Empirical propositions can never be anything more than probable hypotheses, it is only a-prior propositions that are logically certain. But from an a-priori proposition or a set of a-priori propositions the existence of a god cannot be deducted. For a-priori propositions are certain owing to their being tautologies. And from a set of tautologies only further tautologies can be validly deduced. It follows from this that "there is no possibility of demonstrating the existence of a god."[97]

Sometimes it is claimed that it is a sufficient evidence for the existence of a god that there is certain sort of regularity in nature. Ayer argues that "if the sentence "God exists" entails no more than that certain types of phenomena occur in certain sequences, then to assert the existence of a god will be simply equivalent to asserting that there is the requisitic regularity in nature; and no religious man would admit that this was all he intended to assert in asserting the existence of a god. He would say that in talking about God, he was talking about a transcendent being who might be known through certain empirical manifestations, but certainly could not be defined in terms of those manifestations.[98] His argument is "if" god is a metaphysical term, then it cannot be even probable that a god exists. For to say that "God exists" is to make a metaphysical utterance which cannot be either true or false. And by the same criterion, no sentence which purports to describe the nature of a transcendent god can possess any literal significance."[99] The philosophers who believe in the existence of transcendental god, do say that for men it is logically possible to be immediately acquainted with god, as they are immediately acquainted with sense-content. If it is so, then as Ayer has already made it clear, that he does not deny that this assertion may be true. But when they infer from this that there is a transcendental being who is the object of this emotion, then this is what Ayer denies. It is logically impossible to infer a transcendental entity, which is beyond experience, from the empirical assertion. For Ayer, "it is not irrational to be prepared to believe a man when he asserts the existence of a yellow object, and to refuse to believe him when he asserts the existence of a transcendant god. For whereas the sentence "There exists here a yellow-coloured material thing" expresses a genuine synthetic proposition which could be empirically verified, the sentence "There exists a transcendent god" has no literal significance."[100] Thus, Ayer concludes, "the argument from religious experience is altogether fallacious. The fact that people have religious experiences is interesting from psychological point of view, but it does not in any way imply that there is such a thing as religious knowledge, any more than our having moral experiences implies that there is such a thing as moral knowledge. The theist, like the moralist, may believe that his experiences are cognitive experiences, but unless he can formulate his "knowledge" in propositions that are empirically verifiable, we may be sure that he is deceiving himself."[101] In Ayer's opinion these philosophers who are concerned with intuitive knowledge or such moral or religious "truth" are psycho-analysts. For him, "no acat of intuition can be said to reveal a truth about any matter of fact unless it issues in verifiable propositions. And all such propositions are to be incorporated in the system of empirical propositions which constitute Science."[102]

VI

Though Ayer criticises metaphysical doctrine and gives arguments against the possibility of metaphysics, but he has his own shortcomings. Ayer's arguments against the possibility of metaphysics are based on the verification theory of meaning. I agree with Ayer that metaphysical propositions are neither a-priori nor empirical hypothesis. But I do not agree with Ayer that on account of this such propositions are claimed is meaningless. If these propositions are claimed as meaningless because they do not come either in the category of a-priori propositions or in empirical hypotheses, then his own verification theory of meaning is meaningless, for this theory itself is not verified. If it is meaningful proposition, it should be, an Ayer's own premises, either a tautology or an empirical hypothesis. But it is not a tautology, for otherwise no conclusion can be drawn; neither is it an empirical hypothesis, for otherwise this verification principle itself needs verification. Now, if it said, however, that it is not a proposition, then, on Ayer's own account, it would be meaningless. For, according to Ayer's own view, if a sentence, or a statement, or a judgement is meaningful it should express a genuine proposition. It may be said that this is a linguistic proposal or a definition. But, then, it would be purely formal. For in a definition, whether it is expressed in the form of explicit definition or definition in use, the definiens contains nothing but the definiendum itself. In the case of definition in use, the defines is not the meaning of the definiendum, but another symbol or group of symbols which has the same meaning as the definiendum. Indeed, as of metaphysicians Ayer also could not give a clear justification of his theory.

Even granting the theory of verification, the thesis is still not beyond criticism. If we examine Ayer's criticism of metaphysics we find that his argument is nothing more than a tautology. D.M. Datta, in his article *Logical Positivism*, points out, "... if we translate the sentence "Metaphysics is meaningless" by substituting for the subject and the predicate the meanings that they themselves give to these words then it is equivalent to: "That which deals with the trans-empirical (non-empirical) possesses no reference to the empirical." But such a platitude cannot really stultify metaphysics." In his view, a logical positivist "turns positivism into a kind of linguistic solipsism."[103] Ayer's argument against the possibility of metaphysics is similarly applied to ethics, aesthetics and religion. We may agree with Ayer that there is no moral knowledge, aesthetic knowledge or religious knowledge, in the sense that all knowledge is expressed in genuine propositions, i.e. a-priori and empirical. But one may disagree with him that on account of this ethics, aesthetics or religion can be claimed as meaningless. Of course, the ethical statements like "We must tell the truth," "Stealing money is wrong," "Honesty is a moral principle," or religious or spiritual statements like "I am a conscious being," "There is an ultimate reality," "God exist," or aesthetic statements like, "She is charming," "The flower is beautiful," "This painting is good," are not verified by Ayer's verification theory of meaning. But the question is, can moral experience, introspection, religion or spiritual realizations, consciousness, aesthetic experience, be eliminated on account of this? Plainly the answer is "no". We are human beings, due to having such higher experiences. And if we reject them, indeed, we reject our humanity. J.P. Shukla writes, "If such higher experiences are eliminated from the experience of human beings, what is the difference between an animal and a man? All the achievements of science, art and culture become inconceivable and man is reduced to barbarism."[104]

References

1. D.M. Dutta, Logical Positivism, article appeared in *Philosophy-Eastern and Western*, Edited by S. Radhakrishnan, p. 410.

2. "Logical Positivism - a Debate" by A.J. Ayer and F.C. Copleston,

appeared in P. Edward and A. Pap's *A Modern Introduction to Philosophy*, p. 586.

3. J.R. Weinberg, *An Examination of Logical Positivism*, p. 1.
4. *The Encyclopedia of Philosophy*, Vol. V, p. 289.
5. A.J. Ayer, *The Central Questions of Philosophy*, p. 2.
6. A.J. Ayer, *The Central Questions of Philosophy*, p. 4.
7. *Ibid*., p. 5.
8. Kant, *Critique of Pure Reason*, Tr. by N.K. Smith, p. 16.
9. *Ibid*., p. 18.
10. Ayer, *Demonstration of the Impossibility of Metaphysics*, in Mind, 1934.
11. Ayer, *Language, Truth and Logic*, p. 71.
12. Hume, *An Enquiry Concerning Human Understanding*, Sec. II.
13. *Ibid*., Sec. XII, Part III.
14. *Encyclopedia*, Vol. 5, p. 53.
15. *Encyclopedia*, Vol. 5, p. 53.
16. Ayer, *Language, Truth and Logic*, p. 31.
17. Ayer, *Language, Truth and Logic*, p. 79.
18. *Ibid*., p. 87.
19. Ayer, *Language, Truth and Logic*, p. 149.
20. *Ibid*., p. 90.
21. *Ibid*., p. 99.
22. *Ibid*., p. 99.
23. Ayer, *Language, Truth and Logic*, p. 99.
24. *Ibid*., p. 5.
25. *Ibid*., p. 35.
26. Ayer, A.J., *Logical Positivism* (ed.), p. 228.
27. Ayer, A.J., *Logical Positivism* (ed.), pp. 228-229.

28. *Ibid.*, p. 229.
29. Ayer, A.J., *Logical Positivism* (ed.), p. 229.
30. *Ibid.*, p. 229.
31. Otto Neurath, "Protocol Sentences", Erkenntnis, Vol. III, Carl Hemple, "Some Remarks on 'Facts' and Propositions," *Analysis*, Vol. II.
32. Ayer, *Logical Positivism*, p. 230.
33. Vide, *Logical Syntax of Language*, pp. 305-306.
34. Ayer, *Logical Positivism*, pp. 237-238.
35. *Ibid.*, p. 238.
36. Ayer, *Logical Pcsitivism*, p. 240.
37. *Tractatus*, 4.01.
38. Ayer, *Logical Positivism*, p. 240.
39. Ayer, *Logical Positivism*, pp. 240-241.
40. *Ibid.*, p. 242.
41. Ayer, *Language, Truth and Logic*, p. 10.
42. Ayer, *Language, Truth and Logic*, p. 11.
43. *Ibid.*, p. 36.
44. *Ibid.*, p. 36.
45. Ayer, *Language, Truth and Logic*, p. 37.
46. M. Schlick, "Positivism and Realism," Erkenntnis, Vol. I, 1930. F. Waismann, "Logische Analyse des Warscheinlichkeitsbegriffs, " *Erkenntnis*, Vol. I, 1930.
47. *Language, Truth and Logic*, p. 37.
48. *Language, Truth and Logic*, p. 37.
49. *Ibid.*, p. 38.
50. Vide, his logic der Forschung.
51. Ayer, *Language, Truth and Logic*, p. 38.

52. Ayer, *Language, Truth and Logic*, p. 35.

53. Ayer, *Logical Positivism* (ed.), pp. 239-40.

54. Ayer, *Language, Truth and Logic*, p. 45.

55. Ayer, *Logical Positivism*, pp. 64-67.

56. Ayer, *Demonstration of the Impossibility of Metaphysics, Mind*, 1934.

57. Ayer, *Language, Truth and Logic*, p. 42.

58. Ayer, *Language, Truth and Logic*, pp. 42-43.

59. Vide, The Critique of Pure Reason, "Transcendental Dialectic," Book II, Chapter III, Section 4.

60. Ayer, *Language, Truth and Logic*, p. 43.

61. Ayer, *Language, Truth and Logic*, p. 43.

62. P. Edward and A. Pap, *A Modern Introduction to Philosophy*, p. 559.

63. *Language, Truth and Logic*, p. 46.

64. *Language, Truth and Logic*, p. 47.

65. *Ibid.*, p. 47.

66. Carnap, Rejection of Metaphysics, from Philosophy and Logical Syntax, reprinted in A. Smullyan, P. Dietrichson, D. Keyt, and L. Miller's *Introduction to Philosophy*, pp. 21-22.

67. Carnap, Rejection of Metaphysics, from Philosophy and Logical Syntax, reprinted in A. Smullyan, P. Dietrichson, D. Keyt, and L. Miller's *Introduction to Philosophy*, p. 22.

68. carnap, Rejection of Metaphysics, from Philosophy and Logical Syntax, reprinted in A. Smullyan, P. Dietrichson, D. Keyt, and L. Miller's *Introduction to Philosophy*, p. 23.

69. Ayer, *Language, Truth and Logic*, pp. 44-45.

70. *Ibid.*, p. 45.

71. *Ibid.*, p. 45.

72. Ayer, *Logical Positivism* (ed.), p. 22.

73. Frederick Copleston, *Contemporary Philosophy*, Foot-notes, p. 17.
74. Ayer, *Language, Truth and Logic*, pp. 103-104.
75. Ayer, *Language, Truth and Logic*, p. 104.
76. Ayer, *Language, Truth and Logic*, p. 104.
77. *Ibid.*, p. 105.
78. Ayer, *Language, Truth and Logic*, pp. 105-106.
79. *Ibid.*, p. 106.
80. *Ibid.*, p. 106.
81. *Ibid.*, p. 106.
82. Ayer, *Language, Truth and Logic*, p. 107.
83. *Ibid.*, p. 107.
84. *Ibid.*, p. 107.
85. Ayer, *Language, Truth and Logic*, pp. 107-108.
86. *Ibid.*, p. 108.
87. Ayer, *Language, Truth and Logic*, p. 109.
88. *Ibid.*, p. 112.
89. *Ibid.*, p. 112.
90. Ayer, *Language, Truth and Logic*, pp. 112-11.
91. *Ibid.*, p. 113.
92. *Ibid.*, p. 113.
93. Ayer, *Language, Truth and Logic*, p. 113.
94. *Ibid.*, p. 113.
95. *Ibid.*, pp. 113-114.
96. Ayer, *Language, Truth and Logic*, p. 114.
97. *Ibid.*, p. 115.
98. Ayer, *Language, Truth and Logic*, p. 115.

99. *Ibid.*, p. 115.

100. Ayer, *Language, Truth and Logic*, p. 119.

101. *Ibid.*, pp. 119-120.

102. *Ibid.*, p. 120.

103. S. Radhakrishnan, *Philosophy—Eastern and Western* (ed.), p. 429.

104. J.P. Shukla, *The Nature of Mind*, pp. 131-132.

4
Perception

I

Philosophers use the word 'perception' not for mental apprehension, as psychologists do, but they use this word in the sense of 'sense-perception'. "In philosophy it is normally restricted to sense-perception to the discovery, by means of the senses of the existence and properties of the external world. Philosophers have been concerned with the analysis of perception — that is, the study of its nature and of the processes involved in it and with its epistemological value — that is, how far, if all, it can be regarded as a sense of knowledge about the world."[1] The problem of perception has a great importance in the history of philosophy. Philosophers have been struggling hard with this problem since a long time. The questions concerning the problem of perception are, what do we perceive? Do we perceive real physical objects? Do we perceive physical objects as they really are, or what we perceive is other than what they are? Do we perceive them directly or though some representation? How physical objects are perceived by us? Are they perceived by a self or by any substantial entity, or is perception possible without any self? etc. A satisfactory solution of the problem of perception thus, requires an explanation of the nature of physical object and human experience and their relationship.

II

Philosophers have formulated their solutions to these

questions in the form of different theories, such as, common sense theory, theories of direct realism, casual theory, sense-datum theory, and phenomenalism. Although the problem of perception has been of immense importance in all systems of philosophy and yet it occupies a place of paramount importance in empiricism as a whole. In spite of some basic differences between realism and empiricism, philosophers belonging to these two systems of thought devoted their serious efforts towards a solution of this problem.

Realism is opposed to idealism. All realists agree in rejecting the idealistic view that physical objects cannot exist unperceived. They affirm that objects are independent of mind, they exist whether we perceive them or not. Realists themselves differ on the point whether physical objects are perceived directly or by means of sense. Thus realism is distinguished into direct realism and indirect realism. Direct Realism is the general view that perception is a direct awareness, a straightforward confrontation (or being in touch, contact) with the external object.[2] On the other hand, "Indirect Realism claims that perception is primarily of mental representation of the external object, as in traditional representative realism, or that our perception of the external object is by means of private, mental sensa."[3] Direct realism in its simplest form appeared in the Naive Realistic Theory. It is the common sense view of perception. Arthur Pap describes this view in such a way that "Unreflective primitive men assume that the things that they see and touch exist also at times when they are not seen or touched or perceived in any other way; they further take it for granted that things have just those qualities which they appear to have. Let us dignify this unsophisticated creed with the name of native realism.[4]

But this theory of perception is criticized as it fails to explain dream, error and illusion. The assumption of naive realism is generally refuted on the argument from illusion. This argument is based on the fact that physical thing may appear different to different observers or to the same observer in different conditions. To some extent, the character of these appearances is casually determined by the state of the conditions and the observer. The argument given in favour of this view is that physical objects are not perceived directly, but the sense-data are directly perceived. There are several such arguments, but only four important ones are generally considered. In his book 'A Theory of Perception', George Pitcher has arranged them in "an order of increasing persuasiveness."

1. The Argument from Hallucinations

The argument is,[5]

"(a) When a person has a hallucination, he is directly aware of some "sensuous manifold", for it seems to him as if he were perceiving somethings." There are many instances of total hallucination, such as, the drunkard sees pink rates where there are no pink rates, as Macbeth sees a dagger whereas there is no dagger.

"(b) What he is aware of is not objective".

Although a hallucinated person is not aware of any physical object but he must be aware of something, for otherwise what he acts or speaks, he would not.

"(c) Therefore what he is directly aware of is nothing but a sense-datum."

"(d) But what one is directly aware of in normal sense-experience is qualitatively indistinguishable from what he is directly aware of in hallucinatory experiences."

Qualitatively hallucinatory experience is the same as the experience of seeing a real physical object.

"Conclusion: therefore even in normal sense one must always be directly aware of nothing but sense-data."

2. The Argument from Differential Creativity

A figure in a marble museum is mistaken for a real woman, is an example of differential certainty. The argument is[6].

"(a) It is not certain that I see, or that I am, in a visual mode, directly aware of, a (real) tomato, for I could be having a hallucination, I might be the victim of an illusion, someone could have a wax object there to deceive me.....

(b) It is certain that I am, in a visual mode, directly aware of something red and with a tomato-ish shape.

(c) Therefore, the red tomato-shaped somewhat that I certainly am, in a visual mode, directly aware of cannot be identical with a tomato (if, indeed, there is one). It must be sense-datum."

Thus, the conclusion of the argument from differential certainty is, "Since the same sort of argument can be applied in any visual situation, I must always in visual sense perception, be directly aware of nothing but sense data. (Parallel arguments can be constructed for the senses other than vision)."

3. The Argument from Perceptual Realtivity

The argument is:[7]

"(a) Under certain non-standard conditions, things look different from the way they actually are."

There are lot of examples of this type of illusion, as from a distance a large tower looks small or green hills look purple; from an angle, the round coin looks elliptical, the straight looks bent in water, etc.

"(b) In all these cases, something has the apparent qualities. Take the example of the distant hills looking purple: something must be purple, for the perceiver certainly has a purple expense before his conciousness. Something purple is definitely perceived.

(c) But this something is not identical with the physical thing that is being looked at : for example, it is not the distant hills that are purple, for we are supposing that they are really green.

(d) Therefore, the perceiver must be (directly) aware of a (non-physical) representation of the physical thing he is looking at and the perceived quality must in here in this representation. Such a non-physical representation is a sense datum. (similar arguments can be constructed for all the other visually perceived qualities as well)."

Thus physical objects may appear to be what they are not, but it does not imply that we never perceive them as they really are. What it implies is that.

(e) It cannot be maintained that although in non-standard conditions, one is directly aware of the qualities of sense-data, nevertheless in standard conditions, one is directly aware of the (physical) thing itself. If one approaches the distant hills and they gradually stop looking purple and begin to look green, it would be ridiculous to claim that at some point, one stopped sensing the colour of a sense-datum and began to perceive the colour inhering in the hills themselves directly."

The conclusion of the argument is, "Therefore, all qualities we are ever directly presented with in visual sense-perception, even in standard conditions, belong only to sense-data, and so we must always, in visual sense perception, be directly presented with nothing but (visual) sense-data. (Parallel arguments can be constructed for the senses other than vision)."

4. The Argument from the Physiology (or the causation) of Sense Perception

The argument is:[8]

"(a) Science gives us an account of how we see. The Perceiver does not see the object until the impulses reach the brain.

(b) It is the stimulation of certain portions of his brain, then, that is the final stage in purely physical process that causes a person to see things. This brain state either is (i.e., is identical with), or directly causes, a mental act or state - an act or state of (sensuous or perceptual - in particular, visual) awareness.

(c) Part, at least, of this actor state consists in the perceiver's being aware of a sensuous manifold of various colours, lines, and shapes. Since this awareness either is, or is the direct effect of, nothing but the stimulation of certain brain cells, which are of course far removed from the object at the other end of the casual chain. What can it be, but the awareness of a mere representation or image, of the object? But such representations or images can of course only be sense data."

Therefore, again, the same conclusion is drawn by premises that "in visual sense-perception one is always directly aware of nothing but sense-data. (Parallel arguments can be constructed for the senses other than vision)."

Now the question is 'Does argument from illusions refute naive realism? The common opinion is that the view of naive realism is refuted by the argument from illusion. Prof. Price in his chief work Perception does maintain that "The Argument from Illusion is sufficient to refute Naive Realism. This is substantially true."[9] According to him what the argument proves exactly is not very clear, but it has at least this merit to refute naive realism.

According to Ayer the answer of the question, does argument from illusion refute naive realism?, depends upon the way in which the thesis is interpreted. He says, "If one assumes that the naive realist is using the words "see" and "touch" in such a way that to say of an object that it is seen or touched does not entail saying that it exists or that it really has the properties that it appears to have, then the argument from illusion cannot be used to refute him. If, on the other hand, he is using these words in a way that does carry these implications, then the argument does refute him."[10] For Ayer the third possibility "which is suggested by Price's formulation of the thesis is that it should be interpreted as a theory about the analysis of material things in terms of sense-data. And this can be refuted by the argument from illusion."[11]

According to Price's interpretation, naive realists assert that "A is perceiving a material thing, can be analysed into" A is sensing a sense-datum and knowing it to be a part of the surface of X". If it is so, if perceiving a material object can be analysed into sensing a sense-datum and knowing that it is part of the surface of a material things, then naive realism is refuted by means of the argument from illusion. For it is self contradictory to say that the sense-datum by means of which A is perceiving a coin as round, and the sense datum by means of which B is perceiving the same coin as elliptical. Ayer says, "As an argument ad hominem this may be decisive. But all that it proves is that the naive realist's thesis is inconsistent with the conventions of the sense-datum language. So that if we refute him by interpreting his thesis in terms of sense-data we are begging the question against him."[12] According to Ayeı, "we have to regard the naive realism, not as an assertion of fact but as a proposal to use words in a certain fashion; and the same is true of the thesis that we experience sense-data."[13] It is true that the sense datum terminology and the terminology of naive realism are naturally incompatible. If we accept one, we must reject the other. But Ayer explicitly says that "this is not to say that we regard the theory of sense-data as true and the theory of naive realism as false. For these so called theories of perception are not theories at all in the ordinary sense, and therefore the notion of truth and falsehood, which we apply to scientific theories are not applicable to them."[14]

III

According to Ayer the natural heir to naive realism is the causal theory of perception. When people were convinced that there are grounds for holding that we do not perceive physical objects directly, they commonly turned to the causal theory of perception. As we have seen in the consideration of the causal form of the argument from illusion that it is based upon the scientific fact. Ayer says, science proves that "the objects which constitute the coloured, noisy, redolent world of common sense are very much our own creation."[15] Bertrand Russell in An Inquiry into Meaning and Truth says, "We think that grass is green, that stones are hard, and that show is cold. But physics assures us that the greeness of grass, the hardness of stones, and the coldness of show, are not the greeness, hardness and coldness that we know in our experience, but something very different. The observer, when he seems to himself to be observing a stone, is really, if physics is to be believed, observing the effect of the stone upon himself."[16] From this it is inferred that we do not perceive physical objects in their natural states. Arthur Eddington in his book The Nature of the Physical World, represents himself as sitting down at his 'two tables' one of which, as he asserts, has extension, is comparatively permanent, is coloured and above all is substantial, while the other is 'mostly emptiness', relieved by 'numerous electric charges rushing about with great speed."[17] Ayer remarks that "there are two strands of this argument. One is that science corrects the common sense picture of the physical world. The other is that the common sense picture is in any case unlikely to be accurate because of its causal provenance."[18]

The thesis of the causal theory of perception is based upon the acceptance of scientific theory. Its conclusion is derived from the scientific explanation that things are most probably not as they seem to be. The intention of casual theorists is that "they want to distinguish between things they are in themselves and things as they appear to us, and to account as the real properties of physical objects only those properties that they possess independently of our perceiving them."[19] Locke's famous distinction which he drew between ideas of primary qualities and ideas of secondary qualities is commonly allied to the distinction of causal theorists which they attempt to draw between things as they are in themselves and things as they appear to us. Ideas of primary qualities are those of 'solidity, extension, figure, motion or rest, and number.[20] He supposed them to be counterparts of the qualities of the objects which caused us to receive them. The ideas of secondary qualities he thought to be different, such as, colours, tastes, sounds, etc. These ideas are "nothing in the objects themselves, but power to produce various sensations in us by their primary qualities, i.e. by the bulk, figure, texture, motion of their insensible parts."[21] But Locke's distinction of primary and secondary qualities is not the same as the distinction of those perceived qualities which are unaffected by the observer and those which are affected. As Berkeley pointed out in his Principles of Human knowledge, that there is no such distinction, since they are all affected. If it is held that colour is not in the object itself since our sensations of colour are causally dependent upon other factors, such as the state of our nervous system, then similarly it is true for the sensations which he calls ideas of primary qualities. According to Berkeley, "original qualities are inseparably united with the other sensible qualities and not, even in thought, capable of being abstract from them."[23] Moreover, Ayer argues, since all the perceptible properties of physical objects are manifested to us under similar causal conditions, we would appear to have no motive for turning these objects into skeletons, excepted as an act of obeisance to science."[24] According to Hume the causal theory "contains all the difficulties of the vulgar system, with some others that are peculiar to itself."[25]

For Ayer, the decisive objection to the version of the causal theory which turns physical objects into unobservable occupants of an unobservable space is that if this were so we should have no means of identifying them, and if we had no means of identifying them, we should have no reason to believe that they played any part in the production of our sensations, or even that they existed at ail. The point which the advocates of this position have overlooked is that physical objects cannot be identified in the first instance as the causes of our sensations: they have to be independently identified before we can have any right to say that the causal relation holds." It is only because I can, through perception, independently establish the fact that the table is there in front of me, that I can subsequently explain my seeing it in terms of its effect upon me."[26] From this it is followed that "there must be a primitive account of perception which makes no reference to any causal relation between the percipient and the objects which we perceived. This causal requirement can be laid down at a later stage when we have already established our claim to have some knowledge of the physical world. It cannot operate from the start, because the objects which it relates must be independently identified, and since then can be identified, at least in general only through out perceiving them, there must be earlier stages in the analysis of perception in which it does not figure."[27]

Now if it is asked, 'What then becomes of the argument that the causal conditions of perception make it improbable that we ever perceive things as they really are? The answer according to Ayer, is that "it too is out of order: it has no standing at the primitive level. Our criteria of reality have in the first instance to be framed in terms of the way things appear to us. We have nothing else to go by. Only when we have constructed at least an elementary picture of the physical world, can we theorize about it in a way that may make such an argument acceptable."[28]

In this context Ayer examines Russell's assumption, which he assumed in his An Inquiry into Meaning and Truth, that, "Naive realism leads to physics, and physics, if true, shows that Naive realism is false. Therefore, naive realism, if true, is false; therefore it is false."[29] Ayer says, "What physics shows is that the way in which things appear to us is causally conditioned by a number of factors which are extraneous to the thing itself. If, for example, this carpet now looks blue to me it is because light of certain wave-length is being transmitted from it to my eyes, from impulses pass along the appropriate nerve fibers to my brain. In a different light, or if my eyes or brain were injured, it might appear to me a different colour, or no identifiable colour at all. But to infer from this that we do not perceive things as they really are is to make the assumption that if a thing is appearing to have a certain property is caused by outside factors, then it does not really have it."[30] The criteria for deciding what colour things 'really' are, according to Ayer, is "mainly a question of the colour they appear to be under what are regarded as normal conditions."[31] Thus Physics does not refute naive realism, in the sense that it shows it to be false. Physics does not prove that we do not perceive physical objects as they really are. But on the other hand in another sense, physics does refute naive realism. A variant of causal argument proves that light takes time to travel. It is inferred by the argument that in such cases physical objects are not perceived in the state in which they really are. "The sun as we see only as it was eight minutes before; when it comes to remote stars the difference may amount to thousand of years. It may even happen that by the time we see it the star has ceased to exist."[32]

Thus Ayer does agree with the conclusion which is offered by the scientific fact that "we see physical objects only indirectly : what we directly see is something else."[33] And the result of this discussion is that "the arguments so far put forward do not make it excessively uncomfortable to hold the position of naive realism. It will, however, need a little sophistication. We must be prepared to say that we do not always perceive things as they are; that sometimes we see them only as they were, and sometimes as they neither are nor were; that we see, or otherwise perceive, may not exist, or else that we may think that we are perceiving something when we are not in fact perceiving anything at all; and that the physical objects which we do perceive may owe some of their properties in part to the conditions which attend our perception of them. It should derive us, without further argument, into putting up a screen of sense-data between ourselves and physical world."[34]

The theory of indirect realism also took the problem of perception seriously. Descartes maintain that physical objects were perceived through the medium of ideas. John Locke, the principal exponent of representative realism, maintained that we perceive physical objects through the medium of simple ideas of sensation; Berkeley spoke of perceiving ideas and perceiving sensible qualities; Hume substituted the word 'impression' for 'ideas', which are images or concepts of objects.

In more recent times philosophers use the word 'Sense-Data'. An Ayer observes, "as their choice of the term 'idea' indicates, Descartes, Locke and Berkeley agreed in making them subjective, ... They took it to be necessarily true of ideas, in this usage, that they were not accessible to more than one sense, that they were not individually presented to more than one observer, and that they did not exist independently of being perceived."[35]

The word 'sense-datum' was first used as a technical term in philosophy by Bertrand Russell.[36] According to him, "My knowledge of the table as a physical object is not direct knowledge. It is obtained through acquaintance with the sense-data."[37] Russell was greatly influenced by physics. According to him, "When two people look to a given object there are differences between what they see owing to perspective and the way the light falls. There is no reason to single out one percipient as seeing the thing as it is. We cannot, therefore, suppose that the physical thing is what any body sees."[38] theory of perception is much closer to Locke. As Ayer writes "He takes it for granted that all our knowledge of the world is derived from sense-perception, and he also assume that 'the things that are immediately known in sensation' are not straight forwardly identifiable with the physical objects which we ordinarily think that we perceive."[39] He differs from Locke, "in wishing to avoid any suggestion that these elements are mind dependent. So where Locke had spoken of 'simple ideas of sense' - he speaks of sense - data."[40] Russell gives the name of Sense-data to the things that are immediately known in sensation. According to him such things are colours, sounds, smells, hardness, roughness and so on. 'Sensation' is quite different from sense-data. He gives the name of 'sensation' to the experience of being immediately aware of the things. He writes, "whenever we see a colour, we have a sensation of the colour, but the colour itself is a sense-datum, not a sensation. The colour is that of which we are immediately aware, and the awareness itself is the sensation." He says, "if we are to know anything about the table, it must be by means of sense-data brown colour, oblong shape, smoothness etc., which we associate with the table; but for the reasons which we have been given, we cannot say that the table is the sense-data or even that the sense-data are directly properties of the table."[41] If the real table exists, if there is a physical object, a problem arises what is the relation of the sense-data to the physical object.

Russell refutes the thesis of Berkeley who asserts that immediate objects of our senses do not exist independently of us. According to Berkeley there is no such thing as matter at all. He proves that the world consists of nothing but minds and ideas. Commonly we mean by 'matter' something which is opposed to 'mind'. Russell writes, "It is chiefly in this sense that Berkeley denies matter; that is to say, he does not deny that the sense-data which we commonly take a signs of the existence of the table are really signs of the existence of something independent of us, but he does deny that this something is non-mental. — He admits that there must be something which continues to exists when we go out of the room or shut our eyes, — But he thinks that this something cannot be radically different in nature from what we see, and cannot be independent of seeing altogether, though it must be independent of our seeing. He is thus led to regard the 'real' table as an idea in the mind of God."[42]

Since Berkeley and other philosophers have also held that although the table does not depend for its existence upon being seen by me, it does depend upon being seen by some mind the mind of God, or the whole collective mind of the universe. According to Russell, "From the fact that awareness is a state of mind, it does not follow that the things of which one is aware are mental, in any other but the trivial sense of being before the mind, which is just a way of saying that there is no logical reason why sense-data should not exist independently of being sensed. If he nevertheless thinks that they do not so exist, it is on the ground that they are casually dependent on the bodily state of percipient."[43]

Russell takes sense-data as a private entity. Here it is remarkable that on this score what Russell says about sense-data equally applies to percepts. In his article, Physics and Perception,[44] he says "a man's percepts are private to himself: what I see, no one else sees, what I hear, no one else hears; what I touch, no one else touches; and so on. True, others hear and see something very like what I hear and see, if they are suitably placed; but there are always differences. Sounds are less loud at a distance; objects change their visual appearance according to the laws of perspective. Therefore, it is impossible for two persons at the same time to have exactly identical percepts." Russell continues, "It follows that the space of percepts, like the percepts, must be private, there are as many perceptual spaces as there are percipients. My percept of a table is outside my percept of my head, in my perceptual space; but it does not follow that it is outside my head as a physical object in physical space. Physical space is neutral and public. In this space, all my percepts are in my head, even the most distant star as I see it." So, "physical and perceptual space have relations, but they are not identical."

According to Ayer the facts to which Russell draws attention at least make a breach in the position of naive realism.[45] He thinks so to the extent that these facts raise a problem which the naive realism does not attempt to answer. "We think of the physical object as preserving its identity in the various guises in which it appears to us, but exactly how is this achieved? What is it that remains constant while its appearances varies? If the physical object is known to us only through its various appearances, in what way can we distinguish it from them? The naive realist ignores these questions, not because they imply the denial of any doctrine that he holds but because in treating the perception of physical objects as a primitive datum he has already gone beyond them. He has no convenient vocabulary by means of which he can refer to the appearances of things, independently of the things of which we take them to be appearances."[46] But to discuss the relation of physical things of their appearances, such a vocabulary should be needed. And he says, "It is just this that the introduction of the terms like 'sensible quality' or sense-datum has been intended to provide."[47] But Ayer does make it explicit that it does not mean that he is committed to all the implications which their use has been made to carry. What he is suggesting is that something of this sort is needed.[48] Thus Ayer finds many difficulties in Russell's view.

Moore's method to introduce the terminology of sense-data is different from that of Russell. Moore is a common-sense realist, whereas Rusell leads to the causal argument of physics. Thus, Moore introduces sense-datum terminology according to his common sense belief. He explains his usage of the term 'sense-datum' with the help of his famous example of a person who is seeing his own right hand. He writes, "whenever a person is seeing his own right hand as well as something else (e.g. a black background), he must be directly seeing at least two objects: he must, in fact, have a whole visual field, all the objects, in which one is directly seen by him; and, of course, as a rule, the object in this field will be many more than two."[49] For the sake of conciseness he just says, "whenever a person is seeing his hand as well as something else, he must be having a direct visual field which contains at least two objects."[50] And these objects which are directly seen are the examples of 'sense-data'. According to Moore, the sense of the word 'see' in which the objects of the direct visual field are seen is 'visual variety' of what he has somewhere called 'direct apprehension'. Thus he says, "an object is directly apprehended is a sufficient condition for saying that it is a sense-datum. So that according both to my usage and my intentions directly apprehended smells and tastes and sounds are just as much sense-data as directly seen objects."[51] But Ayer points out that Moore" does not say that the fact that an object is directly apprehended is a necessary as well as a sufficient, condition for saying that it is a sense-datum."[52] For otherwise he would be committed to holding the sense-data cannot exist without being perceived, as Berkeley, in his famous principle "esse est percipi", held that a thing cannot exist without being perceived. Berkeley used the term 'perceive' instead of apprehension. According to Moore, sense-data do not depend on the subject for their existence.

In his famous example of a person who is seeing his own right hand, Moore adds a point that this person is also seeing something else. He describes his method of perception as an operation of 'picking-out' a sense-datum. In his 'Defence of Common sense', with the help of the same example he says that this person will be able to pick out something (and unless he is seeing double, only one thing) with regard to which he will see that it is, at first sight a natural view to take, that that thing is identical not indeed, with his whole right hand, but with that part of his surface which he is actually seeing, but will also (on a little reflection) be able to see that it is doubtful whether it can be identical with the part of the surface of his hand in question."[53]

But it is objected by that "if the person to whom one is trying to teach the meaning of the word 'sense-datum' does not understand what is meant by 'a direct visual field' he will not be any wiser; and if he does understand this it is sufficient to tell him that a visual sense-datum is a constituent of a direct visual field, without introducing the complication of a process which turns out to be a process of discriminating between sense-data."[54] Another difficulty in Moore's view is that "he is not prepared to say that the sense-datum is not at any rate part of physical object, since he holds that, in the example in question, it may turn out to be identical with part of the surface of his hands. At the same time he also holds that it may not be very well identical with any part of the surface of the hand and consequently not be even part of any physical object.[55] But it is argued that "if the sense-datum is not necessarily a physical object or part of one, the person who is supposed to 'pick it out' will be likely to require some further indication of the kind of object that it is, and one way of giving him the indication is to show him how certain expressions are being used."[56] Moore himself gives an explanation: "When Macbeth says 'is this a dagger which I see before me?' the sense in which he is using "see" is that which I am now calling "directly see" for it is, it seems to me, obviously the same as that in which we use "see" when we talk of "seeing" an after image with closed eyes."[57] Now it is said that, "this establishes the point that it is permissible to say of something which is not a real physical object, or part of a real physical object, that it is directly seen; and since it is an empirical fact that people do sometimes have visual after image and that they do have visual hallucination, we may infer that there are visual sense-data, in Moore's sense of the term, which are not even parts of any physical objects. We are not, however, entitled to infer that this is true of all visual sense-data."[58] Thus Ayer concludes, "Perhaps, his view is that while it is certain that some sense-data cannot exist without being directly apprehended, it may be the case that others can, just as his view is that while it is certain that some visual sense-data are not parts of the surfaces of physical objects, it may be the case that others are."[3]

Although Moore believes in the reality of sense-data and physical objects and he tries to teach the terminology of sense-data but he feels that he is not sure about the relation of sense-data to physical object.[60]

The same conclusion is drawn due to these difficulties that he could not teach the terminology of sense-data as well.

Ayer regards Prof. Price as the guardian of the theory of sense-data. In his essay entitled Pheno-menalism Ayer writes, "He is not their parent but it is he who has chiefly interested himself in their welfare: it is to him more than anyone that they owe their present position of honour in the philosophical world."[61]

Price teaches this terminology by the method of doubt. Introducing the term sense-data he writes in his book Perception, "When I see a tomato there is much that I can doubt. I can doubt whether it is a tomato that I am seeing, and not a cleverly pointed piece of wax, I can doubt whether there is any material thing there at all. Perhaps what I took for a tomato was really a reflection; perhaps I am even the victim of some hallucination."[62] But there remains something which he cannot doubt. He clearly says, "One thing, however, I cannot doubt: that there exists a red patch of a round and some what bulgy shape, standing out from a background of other colour-patches, and having a certain visual depth, and that this whole field of colour is directly presented to my consciousness."[63] According to him, we may doubt about "what the red patch is, whether a substance or state of a substance, or an event, whether it is physical on psychical or neither, "but can not doubt that "Something is red and round then and there."[64] Here by using the word 'there' he means as he says, "in special relations to other colour-patches presented to my consciousness at the same time."[65] By using the phrase that, it is 'directly' presented to my consciousness, he says, " I mean that my consciousness of it is not reached by inference, nor by any other intellectual process (such as abstraction or intuitive induction), nor by any passage from sign to significate. There obviously must be some sort or sorts of presence to consciousness which can be called 'direct' in this sense, else we should have an infinite regress."[66] Accordingly he asserts, when I am in the situations called 'touching something', 'hearing it', smelling it' etc., in each case there is something which at that movement indubitably exists - pressure (or permanent patch), a noise, a small; and that something is directly presented to my consciousness."[67]

Thus, for Price, the objects of which the existence could not be doubted are 'directly present to consciousness.' Moore uses the phrase 'direct apprehension' for the same purpose. He defines sense-data in terms of 'direct-apprehension'; Price analysis it in terms of 'directly present to consciousness.' According to Price, "This peculiar and ultimate manner of being presented to consciousness is called being given, and that which is thus present is called a datum. The corresponding mental attitude is called acquaintance, intuitive apprehension, or sometimes having. Data of this special sort are called sense-data."[68]

Examining Price's definition Ayer writes, "there is a perfectly good sense in which it can be said that of doubt if this bulgy patch exists. He says, If I were not sure whether the appearances of the patch in question was not a constituent of a dream, it would be entirely proper to describe my situation by saying that I doubted whether the patch existed."[69] Accordingly, he says, "one has to go on to explain that the sense in which it is meaningless to say 'I doubt if this patch exists' is the special sense that is appropriate to sense-data and not to physical objects." And thus Ayer says, "we are once more brought back in a circle."[3] Although Ayer finds some difficulties in Price's method and criticizes him, but he does not deny the contribution which he makes to Oxford Philosophy. In his essay Philosophy and Language,[71] which was delivered as an inaugural lecture as Oxford in November 1960, Ayer says that "the philosophers of my generation are very greatly in his debt." According to him, it was the matter of those Price's lectures which were on Perception, that excited Oxford philosophers.

IV

Ayer accepts the terminology of sense-data, but he introduces the term 'sense-data' in his peculiar way. In his book The Foundations of Empirical Knowledge he stages, "I have not so far attempted to give any explicit definition of the word "sense-datum". I have chosen rather to indicate its usage by giving examples in which sentences referring to sense-data are introduced as translations of sentences the meaning of which is already known."[72] After a discussion of the argument from illusion Ayer remarks, "If I can be undergoing an illusion when, on the basis of my present experience, I judge, for example, that my cigarette case is lying on the table in front of me, I may, in saying that I see the cigarette case, be claiming more than the experience strictly warrants : it is logically consistent with my having just this experience that there should not really be a cigarette case there, or indeed any physical object at all."[73] Therefore he suggests that to give a strict account of one's present visual experience, one must make a more cautious statement. He says, "I must say not that I see the cigarette case, if this is to carry the implication that there is a cigarette case there, but only that it seems to me that I am seeing it." Ayer makes it explicit that here he is not concerned with the question whether such statements are incorrigible. He asserts, "Because of the possibility of illusion, it will not necessarily be true that whenever it seems to me that I am perceiving something, I really am perceiving it. On the other hand, the converse is intended to hold. From the statement that I see the Cigarette case it is supposed to follow that it seems to me that I see it. Or, if this cannot be maintained, it is at least supposed to follow that it seems to me that I see something or other." With the help of the same example, he comes to the next step and converts the sentence 'it now seems to me that I see a cigarette case' into I am now seeming a seeming cigarette case. And then he remarks, "this seeming cigarette case, which lives only in my present experience, is an example of a sense-datum."[74]

Ayer claims to be using the word 'sense-datum in such a way that there can be no serious doubt that sense-data actually are experienced.[75] In following this procedure he gives to the word "sense-datum" the meaning that the philosopher, in general, who adopt the sense-datum terminology, have intended it to have, although he shows clearly that some of the statements about sense-data which they have been made, are inconsistent with this usage. He says "the definition of sense-data that these philosophers commonly give is that they are the objects of which, in sense-perception, one is directly aware." By this definition "the word "sense-datum" is to stand for any object of which it is conceivable that someone should be directly aware." According to Ayer this definition is not illuminating, because "the expressions "direct awareness and "sense-datum" are to be regarded as correlative; and since each of them is being used in a special, technical sense, it is not satisfactory merely to define one in terms of the other."[76]

Another defect of this definition of sense-data is that "it is often associated with the analysis of sensation. According to this view, there are atleast two distinct factors to discriminate in any sensation, that are: (a) the act of sensing and (b) the object sensed. According to Ayer the definition of sense data does not entail this analysis of sensation. He writes, "it is clearly possible to assert that we are directly aware of sense-data without implying that the expression "direct awareness" is a name for any sort of introspectible act." And indeed, he says "it seems to me very doubtful whether there are such acts."[77] Ayer agrees with G.E. Moore, that the expression "blue" and the expression "consciousness of blue" are not synonymous, and that my consciousness of blue and my consciousness of green something more in common than what is common to blue and green.

Philosophers, for the most part use the distinction between act and object in order to refute the theory of Berkeleyan idealism. Berkeley held that all sensible qualities such as colours, shapes, sounds, etc. and mind depended. Their existence consists in their being perceived. According to him, material things are nothing but collections of sensible qualities. Thus material things too, for their existence, depend upon perceiving mind.[78] These philosophers argue that Berkeley falls into error because he does not make a distinction between the act and the object of a sensation. Ayer considers this principle "esse est percipi" or to exist is to be perceived, both in relation to material things and in relation to sense-data. He says, "If the principle that esse est percipi, as applied to material things, is to be interpreted to mean that a logical contradiction is involved in asserting the existence of any material thing that is not actually being perceived, then it is plainly false. For even if it is the case that no propositions asserting the existence of unperceived material things are, in fact, even true, they are still not self-contradictory."[79] The criterion to determine the existence of material things, according to Ayer, "is the truth of various hypothetical proposition asserting that if certain conditions are fulfilled we should perceive it."[80]

One of the purposes of introducing the terminology of sense-data is that "it should enable us to deal with the problems which arise from the fact that material things can appear to have qualities that they do not really have, and can appear to exist when they do not." But this advantage is sacrificed if one extends the distinction between appearance and reality to sensedata themselves. And for this reason he does not allow any meaning to such a sentence as "I am seeing a yellow sense-datum, but it is really brown." Though some philosophers are inclined to attach meaning to such sentences and consider the possibility that sense-data might appear to have properties to which they did not really have. But Ayer says, "by adopting this convention they come to treat sense-data as if they were themselves material things or characteristics of material things; and in that case the terminology of sense-data becomes superfluous. He assets, "There is no point in talking about sense-data of all unless we adopt rules for the use of this technical term that are different from the rules we already follow in speaking about material things."[81]

Ayer holds that the distinction between veridical and delusive perception must not admit with regard to sense-data. He writes, "we must make it a sufficient condition of the existence of a sense-datum that it should actually be sensed."[82]

In holding this view Ayer wishes "to speak not merely of actual but also of possible sense-data; for in analysing propositions about material things we have to refer, not so much to the sense-experiences we are actually having, as to those that we should be having if certain hypothetical conditions were fulfilled. And it may be argued that, in so far as these hypothetical propositions are true. We must allow that possible sense-data also exist without necessarily being experienced."[83] But there is no reason to draw this conclusion. Ayer says, "We do indeed make the truth of these hypothetical propositions a criterion for the existence of material things, but it is not necessary that we should extend this procedure to the case of sense-data. The convenience of our use of the word "existence" as applied to material things consists in the indefiniteness and the generality of its reference. But no such advantage is to be obtained from the proposed usage of "existence" in connection with possible sense-data. There is the disadvantage that the proposed usage, though not indeed identical with that which is adopt inconnexion with a material thing, is sufficiently like it to be a ready source of confusion." This Ayer finds it advisable to make it a necessary as well as sufficient condition of the existence of sense-data that it should in fact be sensed. He says, "only sense-data that are actually experienced will be said to exist."[84]

Ayer also deals with the problem whether sensing is a kind of knowing. He makes a clear distinction between sensing and knowing. If it is essential to knowledge that the object known should exist independently of its knowing then awareness of sense-data can not be a kind of knowing. What is indeed is that it is a necessary and sufficient condition of the existence of sense-data they should in fact be experienced. As he writes, "I am not sure that this is essential to knowledge, as it is ordinarily understood."[85] The reason for this difficulty is that the expression "object of knowledge" is ambiguous. It is used with reference to the knowledge of the truth of proposition, and, on the other hand, it is also used with reference to acquaintance with particular things. Now Ayer says, "If we are concerned with propositional knowledge then there is justification for saying that knowledge presupposes the independence of its object; for it is essential to knowledge of this kind that the truth of the proposition known should not depend upon our knowing it. But it does not follow from this that the existence of a thing which we know, in the sense of being acquainted with it, must also be independent of our knowing it." But this second sense of "knowing" is also ambiguous. For, he says, "we tend to speak indifferently of being acquainted both with sense-data and with material things."[86] To avoid this ambiguity Ayer uses the word "awareness" only in connection with sense-data, the word "perception" only in connection with material things, and the use of the word "knowing" is restricted to its propositional sense. By this distinction it is clear as Ayer remarks that "If one uses the word "knowing" in this way, one cannot say that the awareness of sense-data is itself a king of knowing." But he still says, that it involves knowledge. For "the meaning of the expression "direct awareness" is such that, whenever we are directly aware of a sense-datum, it follows that we know some propositions which describes the sense-datum to be true."[87] But, what is the character of such knowledge? According to Ayer, "In the ordinary way, all that is required for an empirical proposition to be known is that it should in fact be true, and that the belief in it should not have been reached by way of a belief in any false proposition, and should have good inductive grounds; and in this sense we can claim to know propositions about the existence and properties of material things, and even general propositions, although our perceptions can never afford us a logical guarantee of their truth." But it is widely held when we speak of knowing a proposition which describes a presented sense-datum, we imply more than this. It is held that we imply, not merely that our belief in the truth of such proposition is not, in fact, mistaken, but that it could not conceivably be mistaken."[88] Ayer expresses this view by the assertion that such propositions are "indubitable" or "incorrigible."

It is remarkable that the word "indubitable" or "incorrigible" in connection of such empirical propositions, is not used in the same sense as it is used in connection with a-priori propositions. For an a-priori proposition is indubitable in the sense that its contradictory is inconceivable, but the propositions which describe presented sense-data are indubitable on different ground. To assert that proposition describing presented sense-data are indubitable means "to doubt the truth of a proposition which describes a presented sense-datum is logically incorrect."[89] In his view, these propositions are certain they cannot be doubted or they cannot be challenged. In the article entitled Basic Proposions, he writes, "If I make a statement of the form 'I perceived.....' or 'I know ......' or 'I remember ... ', the truth of my statement can be questioned. It may turn out that I was having an hallucination, or that what I claimed to know was false, or that my memory was betraying me. But suppose I merely say 'It looks to me ....', I have a feeling that ...., 'I seem to remember ..... ' How can these statements be challenged? In what could one set about refuting them." It is said that one who says, 'I feel a headache' or 'I feel a pain may be lying. But surely, it is argued, he must know whether he is lying or not. He can deceive others about what he sees or feels. But if his statement refers only to the content of his present experience, how can he possibly be mistaken? How can he even be in doubt as to whether it is true?"[90] He says, "suppose that someone were to tell me 'You think you are in pain but you really are not'. What should I understand him to be saying? Perhaps that nothing was wrong with me physically, that it was all my imagination, or in other words, that the cause of my pain was psychological; and this might very well be true. But it would not follow that I was not feeling pain." When I thought that I was in pain, yet it might be psychological but there is no doubt that I was in pain. According to him, "To suggest to me that I do not feel it may be a way of making the pain stop; but that is a different matter. It does not alter the fact that when I feel the pain, I feel the pain. This is, indeed, an analytic truth."[91] Thus, empirical propositions pertaining to sense-data, such as I feel, I see, etc. are indubitable or incorrigible or certain, because they can not doubted. Ayer calls them "basic propositions." Surely a person may misdescribe his experience, but from this it does not follow that his experience is not incorrigible or indubitable.

To establish his own view Ayer examines other types of empiricistic views. Some philosophers, who maintain that some empirical propositions are incorrigible, assume that "their case would be proved if they could show that the truth or falsity of empirical propositions depended in the last resort, not upon relations that they bore to one another, but upon their accordance with observable facts."[92] So the arguments which these philosophers give in favour of such incorrigible propositions are the arguments against the coherence theory of truth. On the other hand, some philosophers reject this view that there can be such incorrigible propositions appear. Ayer says that what they are anxious to deny is that "any propositions do, or can refer to facts, unless this is interpreted as being merely a misleading way of saying that they have certain relations to other propositions."[93]

Ayer also criticises the picture theory of Wittgenstein, which asserts that propositions are picture of facts. In his Tractatus Wittgenstein writes, "In a picture the elements of the picture are representatives of object."[94] According to Ayer, by asserting this Wittgenstein is able to provide merely verbal solution for the problem. To make his position explicit Ayer analyses the words - sentences, propositions and facts. And he begins with the question, "What does a symbol, for example a word, or a sentence, mean?" There are various ways to answer such a question. "One method," Ayer says, "is that of translation into another language or into an equivalent expression of the same language." For example, "I am thirsty" means "J'ai soif", or "nephew" means "brother's or sister's son". In such cases "it is assumed that the explanatory symbols are already understood by the person for whose benefit the translation is made." Secondly, there is the method of "giving examples to indicate the kind of solution to which a symbol may legitimately be applied." For example, to give the meaning of "jealousy" one may describe it in such a way in which jealous people behave. One may refer to Shakespeare's tragedy of Othello. Finally, Ayer refers to the method of ostensive definition. He writes, "We employ (the method of ostensive definition) when we indicate the meaning of a symbol by correlating it with some perceived object or event."[95] This method is differed from others "in that it does not require any previous understanding of the meaning of other symbols." Ayer clearly says, "It is tempting to think that this method is logically indispensable, which I take to have been the view of those empiricists who denied the possibility of "innate ideas." But this is not so. For it is logically conceivable that people should use words correctly and understand their meaning without any process of learning at all."[96]

According to Ayer, the meaning of a sentence is an empirical fact. And he gives the name of "empirical fact" to whatever can be actually observed. He draws a distinction between directly signified sentences and indirectly signified sentences. And defines the meaning of the sentences of this second class in terms of the meaning of the observation sentences to which, he argues, they are capable of being reduced. In asserting this there are many difficulties. Ayer says, "even if we suppose these difficulties to be overcome, and at the same time set aside the problem of the sentences that are ordinarily held to express a priori propositions by saying either that they too are empirical, or else, more plausibly, that they are not meaningful in the same sense as the others, our theory will still be untenable. .... the meaning of a sentence is independent of the truth or falsity of what it is used to express."[97] For example, he says, "If I say that there is a stove in my room and there is actually no stove in my room, I am expressing a falsehood; if there is a stove, I am expressing a truth; but the meaning of my sentence remains the same, whether or not there is actually a stove in my room. But if it is so, "if the meaning of a sentence is the same, whether what it expresses is true or false, and if in the case where it expresses a falsehood it cannot mean an empirical fact, then it does not mean an empirical fact even when it happens to express what is true."[98] Ayer looks for some other answer to the question. What do sentence mean? To answer this question most of the philosophers invents a class of would be facts, which they call "propositions" According to Ayer, "By doing this they are able to provide a verbal solution for the problem that I am discussing; but the solution is no more than verbal." For Ayer, "What a sentence means is a proposition. These propositions are not capable of being observed; nevertheless it is sometimes held that they are objectively real, even though they do not exist in the way that natural objects exist. But no criterion is given by means of which one could decide when a thing was to be accounted "real". in this non-empirical sense." And the philosophers who called themselves empiricists, when they could not attach any significance to this notion of real propositions, they define the meaning of such symbols in terms of their relations to other symbols. And it is for this reason, as Ayer remarks, that "they fall into the error of formalism."[99]

Now Ayer comes to the point as to why he is required to speak of propositions as well. He says, "the answer is that we often wish to make statements which apply not merely to a given indicative sentence, but also to any other sentences, whether of the same or of a different language, that has the same meaning; and our use of the word "propositions" enables us to do this concisely. Thus, to take a simple instance, he says, "if I say that the proposition" this is red" entails this is not green, I am not saying merely that the English sentence "this is not green" can legitimately be derived from "this is red"; for my assertion could equally well be understood in terms of some other language, such as German or French. It applies not only to these particular English sentences but to any sentences, in any language, that are equivalent to them. And it is this that the use of the word "proposition" conveys." Thus he uses the word "proposition" rather than "sentence" whenever he is concerned with its meaning. Consequently, he says, "we speak of propositions, and not sentences, as being true or false."[100] He asserts that "a proposition is what a sentence means, is, at best, to explain the use of the word "proposition," and is not to make a statement of fact."[101]

After a discussion of what do symbols mean? Ayer deals with the question of How it is possible for symbols to mean? It is assumed by some philosophers that meaning is a relation. Ayer says, "this time the puzzle is not to find the other term of the relation, but to discover the nature of the relation itself."[102] It is asked what is the relation between the word "cats" and cats or between the sentence "this is a pencil" and the fact this is a pencil? Sometimes it is held that the relation is causal, as Bertrand Russell holds in his "The Limits of Empiricism," "What do we know when we know that our words 'express' something we see? I see a cat and say 'there is a cat"? Someone also says 'why did you say "there is a cat?" and I reply, 'because I saw a cat'. The word 'because' must be taken as expressing a relation which is, at least partly, that of cause and effect."[103] There is another answer given by Wittgenstein in his Tractatus that the relation is one of structural identity. He holds,

"The proposition is a picture of reality."

There must be something identical in a picture and what it depicts, to enable the one to be a picture of the other at all.

What a picture must have in common with reality, in order to be able to depict it correctly or incorrectly in the way it does, is its pictorial form.

The configuration of objects in a situation corresponds to the configuration of simple signs in the propositional sign.

In a proposition there must be exactly as many distinguishable parts as in the situation that it represents."[104]

According to Ayer the meaning of a symbol cannot be defined in terms of any relation, i.e. the causal relation, or the relation of structural identity. For "in cases where it expresses a falsehood there is no such fact, and consequently no such relation; and yet symbol is still meaningful. Moreover, even when a symbol does symbolize what is actually observed, it is not necessary that its utterance should be caused by a perception of that which is symbolized, on that it should bear any resemblance to it, whether in structure or content."[105] According to Ayer, "this mistake about the nature of meaning is reflected in the ordinary formulation of "the correspondence theory of truth". For when we are told that a sentence expresses a true proposition if and only if it is used in such a way that it correspond to a fact, we are inclined to interpret the word "correspondence" literally, as implying some sort of resemblance, and then we find themselves confronted with such questions."[106] But he says, "such problems do not arise, once it is made clear that the word "correspondence," if it is used at all in this connection, must not understood literally."[107] How is it, then, to be determined that any empirical proposition does, correspond to a fact? Ayer's answer is that, "in the last resort, it is always to be determined by actual observation."[107] Ayer draws a distinction between propositions which truth is determined directly by observation and propositions which are verified indirectly. He says, "one's ground for believing a given proposition is often, in the first instance, the truth of a second proposition which is evidence for it; and one's ground for believing the second may, in its turn, be the truth of a third; but this series cannot be prolonged indefinitely. In the end it must include at least one proposition that is believed, not merely on the ground that it is supported by other propositions, but in virtue of what is actually observed. In order that we should have reason to accept any of them, it is necessary that at least one of their number should be directly verified by observation of an empirical fact."[108] And a proposition is capable of being directly verified when it is expressed by a sentence the meaning of which is determined by a non-formal rule. If, for example, we have agreed to use the sense-datum language, we shall have to say that propositions like "this is a match-box" or "this is a pencil" are not directly verifiable. For we must hold that the meaning of sentences which express such propositions is to be determined by reference to which designate sense-data, and that it is only when a sentence explicitly designate a sense-data that its meaning is determined by reference to fact."[109] Thus he says, "for a proposition to be directly verifiable, it is necessary that the meaning of the sentence which expresses it should be determined by correlation with some observable state of affairs," though he says this correlation need not be univocal. According to him, "Where the correlation is univocal, as in the case of a sentence which refers to a sensedatum, it is possible to be mistaken about the truth of the proposition expressed, so long as one is not actually observing the relevant fact."[110] But this does not mean that one is "not justified in using it, in view of the evidence which he had. "Ayer clearly asserts, "To be deceived by one's senses is not necessarily to be mistaken about the meaning of words."[111] But there is no such possibility of error when the sense-datum in question is actually being sensed. For in that case the use of the sentence is prescribed by a rule of the language." So, he says "that to make an assertion that does not correspond to the fact is either to tell a deliberate lie or else to make a verbal mistake."[112] And it is for this reason, as Ayer has already held, that sentences of this kind express "incorrigible" propositions.

Ayer also deals with phenomenalism too as a theory of perception. He defines phenomenalism as the philosophical theory which holds that physical objects are logical construction out of sense-data. But in this assertion a phenomenalist does not mean that a physical object is literally composed of sense-data; neither he means that physical object is a fiction and what is real is only sense-data. He simply means that "every empirical statement about a physical object, whether it seems to refer to a scientific entity or to an object of the more familiar kind that we normally claim to perceive, is reducible to a statement, or set of statements, which refer exclusively to sense-data."[113] Ayer says, "What he may be understood to mean by saying that a statement S is 'reducible' to a class of statements K is first that the members of K are on a lower epistemological level than S, that is, that they refer to 'harder' data, and secondly that S and K are logically equivalent." He points out that "the motion of logical equivalence is, in this context, not so clear as one could wish, but it requires at least that it should not be possible to find, or even to describe, a set of circumstances in which one of the statements in question would be true and its supposed equivalent false."[114]

In his article Phenomenalism, Ayer writes that if we confine ourselves to actual sense-data, this claim, i.e. statements about physical objects are somehow reducible to statements about sense-data can evidently not be upheld. For, he says, "to revert to our example, this match box is not continuously perceived either by me or by anybody else. And yet at times then no one is perceiving it, that is, when there are no sense-data that are directly relevant to its existence, the matchbox may still exist."[115] Consequently, he affirms that "if the sense-datum language is to do the work that phenomenalists require of it, it must permit us to refer to possible sense-data." And this means that "some of the statements about sense-data that are supposed to yield the equivalence of statements about physical object will have to be hypothetical. They will have to state not that any sense-data have occured, are occuring, or will occur, but that in certain specifiable conditions certain sense-data would occur."[116]

But the question is, how are these conditions to be specified? Ayer argues that "it is not enough for the phenomenalist to make such vague assertions as that what he means by saying that there is a table in the next room is that if he were there he would perceive it." "For," he says, "his being there is a matter of a physical body's being in a certain spatial relationship to other physical objects, and, on the assumption that to talk about physical objects is always to talk about sense-data this situation must itself be described in purely sensory terms."[117] But in his opinion it is very difficult to see how this could be done.

He further argues, even if one need not mention the observer, one has still place· the situation in which the observations are supposed to be made. One has to describe the setting in which the occurence of certain sense-data is to be taken as establishing the existence of the physical object in question; and this description must be purely sensory."[118] But again he finds some difficulty in this view. He says, "it would seem hardly possible to find a set of sensory descriptions which would sufficiently distinguish one place from another. And when it comes to times the difficulty is even more obvious. Suppose, for example, that the problem were to give a phenomenalist translation of such a statement as that Julius Caesar crossed the Rubicon in 49 B.C. How would one set another rendering 49 B.C.' in purely sensory terms? To this phenomenalist may reply that we do in fact succeed in identifying places and times by making observations; we note features of the landscape, look at watches and calenders, and so forth; and these performances in the end consist in our sensing sense-data." And Ayer remarks, "It does not follow, however, that any description of these sense-data would be sufficient to identify the place or time uniquely; and so long as no such description is found the phenomenalist's reduction has not been carried out."[119]

But from the failure of phenomenalism it does not follow, that "there is no logical connection of any kind between the way physical objects appear to us and the way they really are, He says, There may be no specifiable set of circumstances in which the fact that one does not seem to perceive a certain physical object entails that it does not exist; but given that it is the kind of object that is supposed to be perceptible, it surely would follow that it did not exist if there were no circumstances whatsoever in which it would seem to be perceived. Admittedly, this premise is not one that could ever be conclusively established."[120] For, he points out, "considering the manifold possibilities of illusion, there are few cases in which it even stands much chance of being true. It is a far stronger premise than one would actually require in order to be justified in concluding that some alleged physical object did not exist." The importance of this premise consists in the fact that "in the unlikely event of its being true, the falsity of any statement which implied the existence of the physical object in question would follow as a logical consequence."[121]

He further argues,[122] Just as a statement which implies the existence of a given physical object is not formally refuted by the fact that in a specified set of circumstances the object does not seem to be perceived, so the fact that it does seem to be perceived is not a demonstrative proof that the statement is true. And this applies whatever the particular circumstances may be, and however for the description of them may be extended." But suppose he says, "it were the case that in what appeared to be the relevant setting the object would always seem to be perceived, no matter what further experiences were obtainable." Then, Ayer thinks, "it would logically follow that the object did exist." But again he says, "the premise is not one that could be conclusively established." His assertion is, "There is no object so obstrusive that it could never under any conditions escape one's observation, even though one were placed in the right position for observing it; and this applies even to one's own body." This assertion is based on the possibility of anaesthesia- insensibility of a part of the body.

V

Although Ayer attempts to give an explanation of the problem of perception in consistency with his theory of radical empiricism, his explanation cannot be taken to be entirely satisfactorily. A perception involves three elements of the perceiving subject, the act, and the object of perception. Ayer explains the subject of perception or the self in terms of sense-experience. In fact, he explains both the subject and the object of perception as logical construction out of sense-data, but, as we have already seen, during the course of the discussion of the theory of sensedatum that it fails to do justice to this important problem of knowledge. Ayer holds the view of indirect perception according to which we do not perceive physical objects directly but what we directly perceive are nothing but sense-data which are the objects of direct perception. But his explanation gives rise to two important problems about the nature of logical construction and whether sense-data are mental or physical. Here Ayer fails to explain the exact nature of the logical construction and he also fails to explain whether sense-data are mental or physical. It is because of these difficulties that Ryle calls the theory of sense-data as a logical howler. In the history of empiricism Locke also advocated the theory of indirect perception and yet Ayer's position can be said to be definitely superior to Locke in the sense that it does not contain the enigma of the substance which is not known to us and his explanation is logically more consistent with the doctrine of empiricism. His position ultimately comes very near to the view of David Hume with the difference that in place of ideas Ayer believes in the theory of sense-data. However, credit can be given to Ayer in the sense that he has attempted to elucidate the problem of perception in the light of some recent contributions in this field by the philosophers and psychologists of this century. It can safely be said that although Ayer has not been successful in giving an entirely satisfactory solution of the problem of perception, and yet he has atleast given a good account of the analysis of the problem in accordance with the tradition of analysis initiated by Moore, Russell and Wittgenstein.

REFERENCES

1. *Encyclopedia*, Vol. 6, p. 79.
2. *Encyclopedia*, Vol. 6, p. 78.
3. *Encyclopedia*, Vol. 6, p. 78.
4. Edward & Pap, *A Modern Introduction to Philosophy*, p. 148.
5. George Pitcher, *A Theory of Perception*, pp. 13-14.
6. George Pitcher, *A Theory of Perception*, pp. 113-114.

7. George Pitcher, *A Theory of Perception*, pp. 28-29.
8. George Pitcher, *A Theory of Perception*, p. 43.
9. Price, *Perception*, p. 27.
10. Ayer, *The Foundations of Empirical Knowledge*, pp. 46-47.
11. *Ibid.*, p. 47.
12. Ayer, *The Foundations of Empirical Knowledge*, pp. 47-48.
13. *Ibid.*, p. 48.
14. *Ibid.*, p. 48.
15. Ayer, *The Problem of Knowledge*, p. 113.
16. Russell, *An Inquiry into Meaning and Truth*, p. 15.
17. Arthur Eddington, *The Nature of the Physical World*, p. 11.
18. Ayer, *Central Questions of Philosophy*, p. 83.
19. *Ibid.*, p. 84.
20. John Locke, *An Essay Concerning Human Understanding*, Book II, Ch. VIII, Section 9.
21. *Ibid.*, Section 10.
22. Vide, Berkeley, *The Principles of Human Knowledge*, Sections IX, XV.
23. George Berkeley, *The Principles of Human Knowledge*, Part I, Section 10.
24. Ayer, *Central Questions of Philosophy*, p. 86.
25. Hume, *A Treatise of Human Nature*, Book I, Part IV, Section II.
26. Ayer, *The Central Questions of Philosophy*, p. 87.
27. Ayer, *The Central Questions of Philosophy*, pp. 87-88.
28. *Ibid.*, p. 88.
29. Russell, *An Inquiry into Meaning and Truth*, p. 15.
30. Ayer, *The Problem of Knowledge*, p. 92.
31. *Ibid.*, p. 93.

32. Ayer, *The Problem of Knowledge*, p. 94.

33. *Ibid*., p. 94.

34. Ayer, *The Problem of Knowledge*, p. 95.

35. Ayer, *The Central Questions of Philosophy*, pp. 71-72.

36. Vide, *His Philosophical Essays*, p. 125.

37. Russell, *The Problems of Philosophy*, p. 47.

38. Russell, *My Philosophical Development*, p. 78.

39. Ayer, *Russell*, p. 72.

40. *Ibid*., p. 72.

41. Russell, *The Problems of Philosophy*, p. 12.

42. Rusell, *The Problems of Philosophy*, pp. 13-14.

43. Ayer, *Russell*, pp. 72-73.

44. Russell's article appeared in Edward and Pap's '*A Modern Introduction to Philosophy*,' p. 210.

45. Vide, his *Central Questions of Philosophy*, p. 79.

46. Vide, his *Central Questions of Philosophy*, 79.

47. *Ibid*., pp. 80.

48. *The Central Questions of Philosophy*, p. 80.

49. *The Philosophy of G.E. Moore*, p. 630.

50. *Ibid*., pp. 630-631.

51. *Ibid*., p. 639.

52. Ayer, *Philosophical Essays*, p. 67.

53. *Contemporary British Philosophy*, series II, p. 218.

54. Ayer, *Philosophical Essays*, p. 69.

55. *Ibid*., p. 71.

56. *Ibid*., p. 71.

57. *The Philosophy of G.E. Moore*, p. 630.

58. *Philosophical Essays*, p. 72.
59. *Ibid.*, p. 74.
60. Price, *Perception*, p. 3.
61. *Philosophical Essays*, p. 128.
62. Price, *Perception*, p. 3.
63. *Ibid.*, p. 3.
64. Price, *Perception*, p. 3.
65. *Ibid.*, p. 3.
66. *Ibid.*, p. 3.
67. *Ibid.*, p. 3.
68. Price, *Perception*, p. 3.
69. Ayer, *Philosophical Essays*, p. 129.
70. *Ibid.*, p. 129.
71. Essay appeared in his *The Concept of a Person and other Essays*, p. 1.
72. Ayer, *Foundations of Empirical Knowledge*, p. 58.
73. *The Problem of Knowledge*, pp. 95-96.
74. *The Problem of Knowledge*, p. 96.
75. Ayer, *Foundations of Empirical Knowledge*, p. 59.
76. Ayer, *Foundations of Empirical Knowledge*, p. 61.
77. Ayer, *Foundation of Empirical Knowledge*, pp. 61-62.
78. Vide, *A Treatise Concerning the Principles of Human Knowledge*.
79. Ayer, *Foundations of Empirical Knowledge*, p. 66.
80. *Ibid.*, p. 67.
81. Ayer, *Foundations of Empirical Knowledge*, p. 69.
82. *Ibid.*, p. 70.
83. *Ibid.*, p. 70.

84. Ayer, *Foundations of Empirical Knowledge*, pp. 70-71.

85. *Ibid.*, p. 79.

86. Ayer, *Foundations of Empirical Knowledge*, p. 79.

87. Ayer, *Foundations of Empirical Knowledge*, p. 80.

88. *Ibid.*, p. 80.

89. Ayer, *Foundations of Empirical Knowledge*, p. 81.

90. Ayer, *Philosophical Essays*, p. 115.

91. Ayer, *Philosophical Essays*, p. 115.

92. Ayer, *The Foundations of Empirical Knowledge*, pp. 84-85.

93. Ayer, *The Foundations of Empirical Knowledge*, p. 85.

94. Tractatus, 2.131.

95. Ayer, *Foundations of Empirical Knowledge*, pp. 93-94.

96. *Ibid.*, p. 94.

97. Ayer, *Foundations of Empirical Knowledge*, pp. 95-96.

98. *Ibid.*, p. 96.

99. Ayer, *Foundations of Empirical Knowledge*, pp. 96-97.

100. Ayer, *Foundations of Empirical Knowledge*, p. 102.

101. *Ibid.*, p. 104.

102. *Ibid.*, p. 104.

103. Russell, *The Limits of Empiricism*, Proceedings of the Aristotelian Society, 1935-6.

104. *Tractatus*, 4.01, 2.161, 2.17, 3.21, 4.04 respectively.

105. Ayer, *Foundations of Empirical Knowledge*, p. 105.

106. *Ibid.*, pp. 107-108.

107. *Ibid.*, p. 108.

108. Ayer, *Foundations of Empirical Knowledge*, pp. 108-109.

109. Ayer, *Foundations of Empirical Knowledge*, pp. 109-110.

110. *Ibid*., p. 111.

111. *Ibid*., p. 111.

112. *Ibid*., p. 111.

113. Ayer, *Problem of Knowledge*, p. 118.

114. *Ibid*., pp. 118-119.

115. Ayer, *Philosophical Essays*, p. 133.

116. *Ibid*., pp. 133-134.

117. Ayer, *The Problem of Knowledge*, p. 123.

118. *Ibid*., p. 124.

119. Ayer, *The Problem of Knowledge*, p. 124.

120. *Ibid*., p. 130.

121. Ayer, *The Problem of Knowledge*, p. 130.

122. *Ibid*., pp. 130-131.

5

The Problem of Self

I

The problem of self always remained of central importance in all the different varieties of philosophical thinking and almost every philosopher attempted to provide a solution to this problem. A satisfactory explanation of self becomes still more necessary for the logical empiricists, in the absence of which their aim of the demonstration of the meaninglessness of all metaphysics would not be fulfilled. Although prior to the contemporary thinkers belonging to the trend of logical empiricism, Hume gave a thorough-going treatment of self from the point of view of empiricism. Ayer has also attempted to provide an explanation of the self in consistency with his general philosophical thesis. Like Hume, Ayer also rejects the notion of self as a metaphysical entity in his explanation. For him the self is a "logical construction out of sense-experiences."[1] He explains sense-experience in terms of "sense-contents." A sense-experience is a whole composed of sense-contents.[2] He defines a sense-content not as the object but as a part of sense-experience. For if he defines sense-content as the object of sense-experience he must have to accept the legitimacy of act-object analysis of sense-experiences. And according to Ayer it cannot be legitimate, for it involves the metaphysical assumption of acts of experience. He does not deny that a given sense-content can legitimately be said to be experienced by a particular subject, but that this relation of being experienced by a particular subject is to be analysed not in terms of a substantial self or substantial ego and its mysterious acts, but in terms of the relationship of sense-contents to one another. Another word which Ayer uses in his definition of the self is "logical construction." The relationship between sense-contents and a sense-experience is a relationship of a part and a whole, but the relationship between sense-contents and a logical construction is not the same. He clearly says, "When we refer to an object as a logical construction out of certain sense-contents, we are not saying ... that the sense contents are in any way parts of it, but are merely expressing the syntactical fact that all sentences referring to it are translatable into sentences referring to them."[3]

Ayer distinguishes one object form another by reason of the fact that "it is constituted by different sense-contents or by sense-contents differently related."[4] For him sense-contents themselves are neither mental nor physical. The distinction between mind and matter or mental and physical does not apply to sense-contents, but it applies only to objects which are logical constructions out of them. The criterion to distinguish a given mental object from a given physical object, or a mental object from another mental object, or a physical object from another physical object, is the criterion of distinguishing between different logical constructions whose elements themselves are neither mental nor physical. Sense-contents are parts of sense-experience, but they are elements of logical construction. And being the elements of, the distinction between mind and matter, which is applied only to logical construction, or in other words which are distinctions between logical constructions are reducible to distinctions between sense-contents. But the distinction between mind and matter cannot apply to sense-contents themselves. For, he says, "a distinction between logical constructions which is constituted by the fact that there are certain distinctions between their elements is clearly of a different type from any distinction that can obtain between the elements."[5]

II

The problem concerning the relationship between mind

and matter is nothing more than the linguistic problem which defines certain symbols that denote logical constructions in terms of symbols which denote sense-contents. This problem is not the problem of philosophy. Ayer says "the problem with which the philosophers have vexed themselves in the past, concerning the possibility of bridging the "gulf" between mind and matter in knowledge or in action, are all fictitious problem arising out of the senseless metaphysical conceptions of mind and matter, or minds and material things, as "substances."[6] In this context Ayer considers the question, whether a sense-content can occur in the sense history of more than a single self? The answer which he gives is negative. For he treats a self not as a metaphysical entity, but as an empirical object which is a logical construction out of sense experience, and sense experiences are constituted by the sense contents. In his view, "for any two sense experiences to belong to sense history of the same self it is necessary and sufficient that they should contain organic sense-contents which are elements of the same body." But it is logically impossible for any organic sense-content to be an element of more than one body."[7] Thus all organic sense contents are private in such a way that any of them cannot be element of more than one body.

Here it is remarkable that whether or not one conceives of minds existing apart from bodies but there is still a practice fairly to make a distinction between mind and matter. Ayer himself agrees with the common sense view and makes a distinction between mind and matter. He writes, "even if we cannot allow ourselves to speak of minds as substances, we are able to contrast mental with physical objects or events."[8] One of the principal features of this distinction "is that a privacy which is denied to matter is attributed to mind."[9] Since the word privacy is ambigious as it is used in different ways. Ayer makes it clear in which sense he uses this word. He holds that thoughts and feelings, dreams and imagining, sensations and memories are private in the sense that these are things to which we alone have access. On the other hand, physical objects or events are not private but they are public in the sense that different people do perceive the same physical object. Experiences, either or a public or physical world, or of one's own consciousness, are private to oneself. For, as we have already seen in the discussion of 'sense-data' which are directed 'outwards' towards a public world, are themselves turned 'inwards' by the introduction of sense-data. Two persons perceive the same physical object but these sense-data cannot be the same, although they may be similar. One can communicate his experiences to others but he cannot transfer them to others. Ayer writes, "It is true that one does quite frequently speak of different persons sharing the same thoughts or feelings, but it would generally be held that what is meant by this is that these thoughts or feelings are similar, or proceed by similar causes, not that they are literally the same."[10] But Ayer clearly remarks that the question whether objects are public or private is fundamentally a question of language. In his view, "—— the distinction what is public and what is private depends upon a contingent matter of fact. We do not find it useful to publicize feelings, or sensations or thoughts or images, because they vary so much from person to person; we do find it useful to publicize physical objects because of the extent to which the perceptions of different people agree. But it is not difficult to imagine that two should be on a level or even that the position should be reversed."[11] But Ayer clearly mentions that this is not to say that the distinction which he has drawn between private and public is itself empirical. According to him, when he asserts that experiences are private, he is referring to a necessary truth. This is to say that if someone speaks of the feelings of two different people as they are numerically identical, it would be a contradiction. For it is logically impossible that one person literally feels pain or pleasure of another. He says, "these points of logic are based upon linguistic usages which have the empirical facts in view. If the facts were different, the usage might be changed. These might still be experiences that were not actually shared; but it would not be decided logically that they were unshareable."[12] He maintains that the experiences of a common-experience depends upon the existence of individual experiences. And in maintaining this the claim that one perceives a public object is based on the fact that he has a private experience. The existence of a public object is based on the fact that other people are also disposed to have the appropriate experiences.

Ayer attempts to solve the problem of the seperateness of bodies with the help of the subjectivity of sense-contents. He asserts, "it is logically impossible for any organic sense content to be an element of more than one body." Disagreeing with the above argument, C.E.M. Joad writes, "I find it difficult to avoid the conclusion that in making this statement Ayer has inadvertently reintroduced the familiar notion of the body as a physical thing. It is because one physical thing cannot be other physical thing, that he tells us that "it is logically impossible for any organic sense-content to be an element of more than one body." In other words, it is not so much a logical impossibility that is involved here, as a physical impossibility. But the notion of a physical impossibility entails the notion of a body as a physical thing. And, indeed, it is precisely this notion, the notion of the body as a physical thing to which Ayer remarks when he is off his guard. If, however, the actions of other people's bodies are to be interpreted solely in terms of the sense-contents of those who observe them, these afford us no reason to believe in any thing but the occurence of the observer's sense-contents, no reason, therefore, to believe in other people's bodies, and no reason to believe that the owner of these bodies understands Ayer's utterances."[13]

Ayer analyses the notion of the self in terms of those sense-contents which are elements of the same body. According to C.E.M. Joad, "This either presupposes the dogma that all experiences are sensory experiences which originate in occurrences in the body, or, if other kinds of experiences are admitted, excluded them from the series of those experiences which constitute the self. Now, the view that all experiences are sensory is both universified and universifiable. Let us suppose for the sake of argument that there is such a thing as a non-sensory experience; we will suppose, for example, that my experience of reflecting on Lord Acton's dictum to the effect that all power corrupts is what is prima facie seems to be, a non-sensory experience. It follows, presumably, on Ayer's view, that it does not belong to the self which I regard as mine, since it does not "contain organic sense-contents which are elements of the same body." Hence, the self which Ayer concedes is a self which eats and sees but is not a self that calculates and thinks. This view seems to contradict the testimony of all those who have seemed to enter most fully into themselves in the experience of active moral struggle or of meditation and contemplation. To exclude such experiences, from the definitions of the self seems to be wholly arbitrary. It also excludes the self which thinks Ayer's thoughts and expresses them in his books."[14] Similarly this objection of solipsism is raised by Stebbing.[15]

Ayer himself was aware that his account may be deemed to be solipsistic. He says, "It will be said that anyone who maintains both that empirical knowledge resolves itself on analysis into knowledge of the relationships of sense-contents, and also that the whole of a man's sense-history is private to himself, is logically obliged to be a solipsist that is, to hold that no other people besides himself exist. For it follows from his premises, so it will be argued, that the sense-experiences of another person cannot possibly form part of his own experience, and consequently that he cannot have the slightest ground for believing in their occurence: and, in that case, if people are nothing but logical constructions out of their sense-experiences, he cannot have the slightest ground for believing in the existence of any other people."[16] So he defends himself against this charge. He denies that it is a necessary consequence of his epistemology. Solipsism is rejected by him for the reason that it contradicts the basic assumption of his analysis of the self. For his analysis is not restricted to oneself, but he considers other selves as well. Ayer interprets the experiences of others as well as one's own in terms of the behaviour of their bodies. As he says, "Just as I must define material things and my own self in terms of their empirical manifestations, so I must define other people in terms of their empricial manifestations that is, in terms of the behaviour of their bodies, and ultimately in terms of sense-contents.[17] Since the concept of experience is similarly applicable to others as well as to oneself, he is logically led to give the same behaviouristic interpretation of one's own experience as that of others.

III

Ayer deals with the problem about one's knowledge of other minds in his Philosophical Essays. In dealing with this problem Ayer considers the following propositions:

"(1) When some one other than myself, says that he has a headache, what he is saying about himself is the same as what I should be saying about myself if I were to say that I had a headache.

"(2) When I say someone other than myself that he has a headache, what I am saying about him is the same as what I should be saying myself if I were to say that I had a headache.

"(3) When I say that I have headache my statements is not equivalent to any statement, or set of statements, however complicated about my overt behaviour.

"(4) I have direct knowledge of my own experiences.

"(5) I cannot have direct knowledge of anyone else's experiences.

"(6) Consequently, the ground that I can have for believing that other people have experiences, and some at least of their experiences are of the same character as my own, is that there overt behaviour is similar to mine."[18]

As his starting point, Ayer takes the propositions that "I have direct knowledge of my own experiences" and," I cannot have direct knowledge of anyone else's." He analyses these propositions in such a way that "the knowledge claimed is knowledge that something is the case, that I have a headache: and the point is that if the statement which expresses what I claim to know refers only to my present experience, I am in the best possible position to decide its truth. If I judge it to be true, it is on the basis of an experience which conclusively verified it, in as much as it is the experience which the statement describes. Let it be granted that others besides myself can come to know that such a statement is true. Even so, their knowledge will not be direct. For it can be founded only upon experience of their own, and however strongly these experiences favour the truth of the statement about my experience, they do not establish it conclusively. It remains at least conceivable that these experiences should occur and the statement in question is false. But no such possibility of error arises when an experience testifies only to itself."[19] Thus he says, "the warrant for saying that I can have direct knowledge of my own experiences but not of anybody else's is just that my experiences are exclusively my own. The reason why I cannot directly know the experiences of another person is simply that I cannot have them."[20] And if it is said that two different people may perceive the same object, or hear the same sound, but as we have already seen, they may perceives the same object or hear the same sound, they cannot sense the same sense-data. Their sense-data may be qualitatively similar but numerically cannot, in such a way that there are two feelings and not one, for they are two persons and not one. And for this reason it is asserted that any feeling which one has, is an experience which is private to oneself. So he takes it as a necessary fact that one cannot have the experiences of others. But in asserting this necessary fact that one cannot have the direct knowledge of others, he does not mean that one cannot inspect thoughts or feelings or sensations of others. Experiences are private to oneself in the sense that only he has them but he can display them to anyone else.

We know about the experiences of others in such a way that either they are communicated to us by the use of language or by their natural manifestations such as tears, laughters, gestures, play of features and so on. I know the experiences of another person only by inference. But the question is whether and how this inference is justified. The usual answer to this question is that it is justified by an argument from analogy which is based on the fact that there is a perceptible resemblance between the behaviour of other bodies and that of its own.

Ordinarily, an argument from analogy is a substitute for direct observation. Ayer gives an instance, and writes, "suppose that the symptoms of two diseases are similar in certain respects and I have discovered that one of the diseases is caused by a microbe of a certain sort; I may infer my analogy that the other disease also is caused by a microbe which I have not so far observed, and I may then set about trying to detect it."[21] Ayer says, "I can legitimately use an argument from analogy to establish the probable existence of an object which has never in fact manifested itself in my experience."[22] But in the case of other minds there is nothing describable as detecting the thoughts and feelings of another apart from adding to the premises of the argument, that is, collecting further information about this behaviour."[23] As it is already asserted by him, it is not logically possible that the experiences of other people can occur in one's sense-history and if it is so, the argument for analogy cannot have any application regarding the existence of these experiences. Ayer says, "By analogy with what I have observed of other people and what I have learned about myself, I infer that someone with the relevant sort of nervous system, when operated on in such and such conditions, will show signs of pain, signs that I may well be able to detect if I watch him closely enough. But when I want to go further and argue from the existence of these signs to the existence of his actual feeling of pain, which ex hypothesi, since it is not my feelings, I cannot detect."[24] Now he comes back to the first of the propositions which is listed by him. 'When someone other than myself says that he has a headache, what he is saying about himself is the same as what I should be saying about myself if I were to say that I had a headache.' He remarks, "A shorter and more familiar form of this proposition is: 'When someone other than myself says "I have a headache" what he means in the same as what I mean when I say "I have a headache"'. But when it is put in this way, there is likely a sense in which the proposition is false. For when he says, 'I have a headache' he means that he has a headache, and when I say 'I have a headache' I mean that I have a headache, and since we are two different persons our meanings are not the same."[25] However there is a sense in which their meanings are the same. For if we both are using English language correctly, he uses the words 'I have a headache' only to state that he has a headache and not to state something else, as he has a headache, similarly I also use the words 'I have a headache' only to state that I have a headache, and not that I have a toothache or anything else. Thus Ayer asserts, "Rules can be given for the correct use in English of expressions like 'I have a headache,' and these rules are intersubjective in the sense that not only I but any one can follow them. Thus the reason for saying that what my friend means when he says that he has a headache is the same as what I mean when I say that I have a headache is that our use of expression 'I have a headache' confirms to the same rules."[26]

The next proposition in his list is that, "when I say someone other than myself that he has a headache what I am saying about him is the same as what, I should be saying myself if I were to say that I had a headache." And the reason for this saying again is that "it is the same in so far as the use of the expression he has a headache is governed by the same rules as the use of the expression 'I have a headache.' There are, indeed, peculiarities about the use of personal pronouns, especially in the first person, which make these two expressions function somewhat discrepantly; but there is still a sense in which they may properly be said to confirm to the same rules."[27] And he says, just as my saying that I have a headache and my having in certain ways is good evidence in favour of my having a headache, and none the less good because I myself do not require it, so his saying that he has a headache and his behaving in certain ways is good evidence in favour of his having a headache, and none the less good because he does not require it."[28] But it is to be noted that though the evidence is good but it is not conclusive. Thus, in the end he asserts the proposition, "the only ground that I can have for believing that the people have experiences, and some at least of their experiences are of the same character as my own, is that their overt behaviour is similar to mine."

In this way Ayer interprets the experiences of others as

well as one's own in terms of their bodily behaviour. But in his Language, Truth and Logic, he clearly says, "Each of us must define the experiences of others in terms of what he can at least in principle observe, but this does not mean that each of us must regard all the others as so many robots. On the contrary the distinction between a conscious man and an unconscious machine resolves itself into a distinction between different types of perceptible behaviour. — when I assert that an object is conscious I am asserting no more than that it would, in response to any conceivable test, exhibit the empirical manifestations of consciousness. I am not making a metaphysical postulate concerning the occurence of events which I could not, even in principle, observe."[29]

Ayer does not give any definition of consciousness. He speaks of it in the ordinary sense, according to which "to be thinking about a problem, or remembering some event, or seeing or hearing something, or deciding to do something, or feeling some emotion such as jealousy or fear, entails being conscious."[31] He does not commit himself to any view in which the notion of consciousness would be analysed. In this sense, the characteristic of a person, mas Ayer says is that, "besides having various physical properties including that of occupying a continuous series of spatial positions throughout a given period of time, they are all credited with various forms of consciousness."[31] In his Concept of a Person, Ayer deals with the question as to how these manifestations of consciousness are related to the physical attributes which also belong to persons. There are different views about it, but they are mainly of two forms i.e. the form of dualism and form of monism. Dualistic view is mainly associated with Descartes. According to this view a person is a combination of two different or separate entities, a physical body and a conscious mind or self or soul. Only mind is conscious, the physical properties of a person are the properties of his body. Physical body and conscious mind or self are separate in the sense that there is no logical connection between them. It is not contradictory to suppose that a person's self or mind exists in some other body or without any body at all, or a persons's body is animated by some other self or without any self at all. Descartes believed that in being self-conscious one is aware of a spiritual which is housed contingently and perhaps only temporarily in the body.[32] According to Ayer this view is untenable. He accepts, with common sense that the relation between body and mind is not logical but only factual. To say that there is no logical connection between them, Ayer argues, "this does not exclude the possibility of there being causal connection between them; so that even if they are separable in principle, there may still be grounds for holding that they are inseparable in fact."[33] According to him the reasons why the observer or person associates his percepts with the central body are chiefly causal. A person "notices that tactual percepts occur only when the objects to which the tactual properties are assigned are in contact with some part of this body; indeed, there is a way in which they are also located in the body. The same double location is characteristic of percepts which belong to the sense of taste." Ayer says, "When it comes to the data of the other senses, the causal connection is not quite so obvious, but it is not very hard for the observer to correlate variations in these data with movements of the body."[34] Another relevant fact, in his view, is that "the part played by his body is found to a greater extent to be under his control. Thus, the presence of light is a constant condition of the occurance of his visual percepts."[35] Further, "It is also of importance that the observer's identification of himself goes together with his identification of other persons and with their identification of him. He regards the central body as belonging to him in the special way in which their bodies belong to them, and he thinks of his body not only as a contributory cause of his percepts but also as the medium through which his entertainment of them, and indeed of his experiences in general, is made known to others."[36] Finally, "the association of his percept with his body is reinforced by the fact that many, if not all, of them are sensibly compresent with bodily sensations. It is arguable that even when these sensations do not obtrude themselves upon one's notice, they are usually present in the form of a relatively constant background to more interesting items of experience. Moreover, even if we allow that some percepts are not accompanied in this way by bodily sensations, it is very probable that they will be sensibly continuous, at one or more removes, with percepts which are so accompanied."[37] On account of this, Ayer thinks, "it would be compatible with this sort of dualism to reject the notion of mental substance altogether and conceive of the mind, in Human as a series of experience."[38] Here again, it is to be noted that though Ayer is not fully satisfied with Hume's analysis of the self but there is no doubt that he is greatly influenced by him.

Though for common sense, the dualistic view is more attractive but because of some serious difficulties philosophers attempted to give alternative formulations more in the form of monistic view. Berkeley placed his view in the form of a spiritual type of monism. He rejects the independent existence of physical objects and held that physical objects were nothing but collections of sensible qualities which were dependent upon being perceived for their existence. He formulated his view in "esse est perceipi" (to exist is to be perceived). Hume did not find any ground for holding the existence of anything but sensory impressions and ideas which copied them in their different ways. According to Ayer, he "tried to effect the reduction of body to mind."[39] In more recent time the theory of monism has developed in its peculiar manner by William James and Bertrand Russell, who take sense-data and images as fundamental. In Ayer's view, they are held to constitute a kind of natural stuff, itself neither mental nor physical, out of which both mind and matter are to be constructed."[40] On the other hand, Hobbes did not need to postulate the existence of mind in addition to body. According to him, conscious states and activities could be attributed to the body itself. In contemporary period some philosophers like Gilbert Ryle, Rudolf Carnap etc. reject the existence of any conscious self or mind. Their views are of the physicalistic type of monism. According to them, statements about person's mental life reducible to statements about their physical constitution, or in other words, to their actual and potential behaviour.

IV

An important problem pertaining to any theory of mind is that of personal identity. Philosophers belonging to the different shades of thought took interest in trying to provide a satisfactory solution of the problem of personal identity. What is more important is that no philosopher denies the truth of personal-identity, and they all try to give varied explanations of personal-identity. Quite often their interpretations differ show radically from each other that sometimes it appears to a philosopher belonging to one particular type of thinking that the interpretations that are given by others appear as the denial of personal identity. For a dualistic view, an account is required of the way in which the mind is lodged in the body. Could there be more than one mind in a single body? Could the same mind dwell in more than one body, at the same or at different times? If the relation is one to one, how are its items paired off? How is it decided which mind goes with which body?"[41] Mostly, the answer is given that in some special way mind and body are causally connected, but then the question is how this connection is to be identified. Ayer says, If the mind is regarded as a substance the question arises how such a substance could ever be identified. It is regarded as a collection of experiences, there is the problem to which Hume himself confessed that he could see no answer,.of showing how the collection is united. What is it that makes a given experience a member of one such collection rather than another?"[42] The problem of identifying experiences themselves corresponds with any view of this type. If we identify experiences in terms of the persons whose experiences they are as we do in ordinary way, Ayer remarks, "this will lead to a vicious circle is persons themselves are to be analysed in terms of their experiences."[43]

The difficulty about personal identity does not remain so intricate for the physicialistic type of monism. For, by apply the same criterion, by which it determines the identity of their bodies, it will solve the problem of the identity of persons. Ayer says, "if, persons can be equated with their bodies, there will no longer be any need to specify how minds and bodies are correlated. Once it is shown how states of consciousness can be ascribed to bodies, this problem will have been solved."[44] But it is itself an open question, whether this can be shown? The physicialists deny the existence of mental as opposed to physical events. They do not deny that people think or feel or act or perceive things through their senses but in their views all these processes can be analysed in purely physical terms. According to this theory the concept of a person is derivative, for it is capable of being analysed into simpler physical elements. In an ordinary way, physicialists maintain that propositions which refer to mental states and processes are logically equivalent to propositions which refer to people's overt behaviour, they differ themselves only about the character of such elements and the way in which these elements are combined.

In recent years, Ayer has remarked that the premises that concept of a person is denivative has been challenged by some philosophers. Strawson has attempted to prove, in his book Individuals, that the concept of a person is a primitive concept, it cannot be analysed in terms of physical elements. But by maintaining this he does not mean that a person is a product of two separate entities mental, which is the subject of consciousness and physical, which is the subject of physical characteristic. For he holds that the subject to which one attributes the properties of consciousness is literally identical with that of the subject to which one attributes physical properties. Ayer says, "If we ask what this subject is, the only correct answer is just that it is person."[45] Strawson rejects the theses of dualism on the ground that "the concept of the pure individual consciousness the pure ego is a concept that cannot exist; or, at least, cannot exist as a primary concept in terms of which the concept of a person can be explained or analysed. It can exist only if at all, as a secondary, non-primitive concept, which itself is to be explained, analysed in terms of the concept of a person."[46] Here it may be said that dualism is not rejected by this. For, though he rejects the notion of the pure ego, but thinks of the conscious subject as a collection of experiences. But, as Ayer says "in fact the reasons which Mr. Strawson has for denying that there can be a primary concept of the pure ego apply equally to any idea of a non-physical subject of consciousness."[47]

The first premises of Strawson's argument is : "That it is a necessary condition of one's ascribing states of consciousness, experiences, to oneself, in the way that one does, that one should also ascribe them, to be prepared to ascribe them, to others who are not oneself."[48] This excludes the view which holds that the statements are to be analysed quite differently which one makes about the experiences of others from the statements which one makes about one's own. According to this view in the case of other's experiences one can be constructed the statements only as a reference to their behaviour, but in the case of one's own, one is to be understood as speaking literally. Ayer attempted to justify the position. He says, "An important consequence of this argument, if it is sound, is that we must give up the argument from analogy on which many philosophers have relied as a justification for believing in the existence of other minds. It is tempting to think that one can come by the idea of one's own experiences of certain kinds are characteristically associated with certain forms of behaviour, and so, when one observes other people behaving in similar ways, infer that they are having similar experiences. Even if one does not acquire the belief that there are other minds in this fashion, it may still be the ground for holding that the belief is rational."[49] But there are various objections against this reasoning. According to Ayer, as we have already seen, it is logically impossible that one can directly observe what goes on in the mind of another person. It is also said that there is no inductive argument which can give us any reason to believe in the existence of anything which could be observed even in principle. Therefore, this argument is invalid. Some other philosophers assert that the basis of this argument is very weak, as Wittgenstein argues in his Philosophical Investigations, "how can I generalise from the one case so irresponsibly?"[50] Strawson himself denies the validity of the argument from analogy. Ayer writes, "The novelty of Mr. Strawson's attack lies in his refusal even to allow the argument to start. If my knowing how to ascribe experiences to others is a necessary condition of my being able to ascribe them to myself, then, Mr. Strawson suggests, the argument begins by presupposing what is intended to justify."[51] He maintains that it is circularity in the argument from analogy for it justifies the belief that there are other persons by relying on the premises that one knows oneself to be a person. It would be circular for what argument is supposed to prove would be already assumed in the premiss. Now Ayer argues that "It is the conditions of being a person unless I admitted the possibility that others satisfied them too. But all that this excludes is the view, which has indeed been held by some philosophers, that it is meaningless to ascribe states of consciousness to anything but oneself, it is perfectly compatible with the view that one cannot know, that such an ascription is ever true in fact. But if I can know that I am a conscious subject without knowing that there are any others, there need be no circularity in an argument which proceeds from the premiss that I have experiences and arrives at the conclusion that others have them also." Here it may be objected, as Ayer himself remarks, that "when it is said that I must be prepared to ascribe states of consciousness to others in order to be able to ascribe them to myself, I must already believe that I can be justified in ascribing experiences to others before I can significantly ascribe them to myself, and in that case an attempt to base this justification on my knowledge of my own experiences will be circular."[53] Ayer gives an answer to this question by stating that "there is a difference between my believing that I am justified in accepting a given position and my really being so; and not only that but a relief in a proposition may be justified without the proposition's being true. So even if I could not think of myself as a person unless I also thought that I had reasons to think of the same of others, I could still consistently raise the question whether these reasons really did the work that was required of them, and even if I were able to decide that they were good reasons, I still should not be bound to hold that they were conclusive."[54] Therefore he thinks that the argument of Strawson needs a stranger premiss than the one that he needs. He says, "It must hold it to be a necessary condition of one's ascribing states of consciousness to oneself not merely that one should ascribe them, or be prepared to ascribe them, to others, but that one should be sure of doing so successfully. It, must in other words, exclude the possibility of one's being invariably mistaken."[55]

According to Ayer the difficulty with the argument from analogy is that any inductive argument allows for its conclusion to be false. So he says, "if my belief that other beings are conscious can be defended only as an inference from their behaviour, it is at least possible that I am the only person in the world. The short answer to this is that I know that I am not; but this still leaves the problem how I can have the right to be so sure. If physicialism were true, this problem would give no trouble, but I do not see how the obvious objections to physicialism are to be overcome."[56] Therefore Ayer says, "I am inclined to agree with Mr. Strawson that we ought to try to find a middle way."[57] Strawson does not accept the thesis of physicialism, which holds that statements of experiences are transformable into statements about physical occurances, instead of this he is concerned with the theory which he calls the 'no-ownership' doctrine of the self. Ayer says, "This is the theory that the only sense in which experiences can significantly be said to have an owner is that they are causally dependent upon the state of some particular body."[58] Since Ayer prohibits this disembodied existence of a person, he argues against his view. He says, "The experiences which might then ensue may themselves be imaginable; but it would seem that in crediting them with an owner we are making a tacit reference to body which is supposed to have been forsaken."[59] According to him "Mr. Strawson's idea appears to be that one could retain one's identity through having memories of one's former life. But here he seems to have forgotten that something is needed to secure one's continued existence as a person; and for this we have seen that memory will not suffice."[60] To avoid these difficulties Ayer writes, "I am inclined to think that the personal identity depends upon the identity of the body, and that a person's ownership of states of consciousness consists in their standing in a special causal relation to the body by which he is identified. I am not maintaining, of course, that this is how one actually becomes aware of one's own experiences, but only that the fact that they are one's own, or rather the fact that they are the experiences of the person that one is, depends upon their being connected with this particular body."[61]

In this connection, Ayer considers the view of Professor Hampshire too, who suggests that persons are to be distinguished by their capacity of action. In his book Thought and Action, Hampshire says, "The deepest mistake in empiricist theories of perception, descending from Berkeley and Hume, has been there presentation of human beings as passive observers receiving impressions from "outside" of the mind where the "outside" includes their own bodies. In fact, I find myself from the beginning able to act upon objects around me I not only perceive my body, I also control it; I not only perceive external objects, I also manipulate them. To doubt the existence of my body would necessarily be to doubt my ability to move ...... I find my power of movement limited by the resistance of objects around me, in conjunction with my perceptions, my own situation as an object among other objects."[62] Hampshire thinks so, according to Ayer, only because "persons are themselves physical objects with a situation in space and time and with a power of movement which brings them into constant with other physical objects, including other persons with whom they can communicate, that they can even form the idea of an objective world."[63] According to him, personal identity can be defined in terms of human action. He says, "We have no reason to seek for some criterion of personal identity that is distinct from identity of our bodies as persisting physical objects. We find our intelligence and our will working, and expressing themselves in action, at a particular place and a particular time, and just these movements, or this voluntary stillness, are unmistakably mine, if they are my actions, animated by my intentions I can only be said to have lost a sense of my own identity if I have lost all sense of where I am and what I am doing."[64] According to Ayer the analysis of predicates which are concerned with human action does not provide the answer to the problem of self-identity. He says, "Professor Hampshire may well be right in claiming that even in our infancy we are not simply the passive recipients of sensory impressions; it may be true that one comes to think of oneself as an object among other objects through feeling the resistance which these other objects oppose to one's will. But this fact, if it be a fact, about the way in which a person acquires the idea of his own identity does not tell us in what this identity consists."[65]

In rejecting the thesis of physicalism Ayer does not come back to the dualistic position of Descartes. He clearly says, "It is possible to hold that states of consciousness are distinct both from their physical causes and from their physical manifestations, without being obliged to hold that there is a mental substance to which they are ascribable."[66] Neither does he commit himself to the position of Hume.

Hume rejected the entity of a substantial self on the ground that there is no such entity which was observable. For, he said, whenever he entered most intimately into what he called himself, he always stumbled on some particular perception of other — of heat or cold, light or shade, love or hatered, pain or pleasure. He never could catch himself at anytime without a perception and never could observe anything but perception. Thus he asserted that a self was "nothing but a bundle or collection of different perception."[67] But Hume had to face the problem of personal identity. He did not find any relation between perceptions in virtue of which they formed a single self. He himself admitted in his Treatise of Human Nature that "all our distinct perceptions are distinct existences, and the mind never perceives any real connection among distinct existences. Did our perceptions either inhere in something simple and individual, or did the mind perceive some real connection among them, there would be no difficulty in the case."[68] Ayer says, "Since he believes that neither of these conditions is satisfied, Hume is obliged to 'plead the privilege of a sceptic' and leave the problem unsolved."[69] Ayer agrees with Hume in saying that our distinct perceptions are distinct existences in the sense that they are logically independent. We can describe the nature of one perception in such a way that it does not entail anything about the nature of the other. But, in his view, it does not follow from this that they are not factually connected. Ayer says, "there are gaps in consciousness of which we have to take account. When I wake from what I take to have been a dreamless sleep and the fact that I do so take it is sufficient to break the sensible continuity, whether or not it really has been so - I have no doubt that I am the same person as went to sleep so many hours before."[70] But he argues, "what is it that unites my present experiences with those that I had then?" It may be answered that they are joined in memory. But, in his opinion, this answer is not correct. He says, "It is, indeed, through memory that I discover myself identity over the period of time, but it cannot be memory that produces it. The reason why it cannot is that if we take the assumption that the experiences which I think that I recall cannot fail to have been my own. We are reasoning in a circle; and if we do not make this assumption, the link is not established; the experience in question might never have been occured, or they might belong to a different biography."[71] Therefore, Ayer comes to the fact of bodily identity. According to him, "My present experiences and those that occured before the interval of unconsciousness to the same series because they are alike compresent with percepts which are associated with the same body."[72] But to claim that memory is not sufficient to bridge a gap in sensible continuity he does not mean that it carries no weight at all. What he wants to assert is that only memory is not sufficient but bodily identity is also needed. In his work The Problem of Knowledge, Ayer clearly asserts, "We have not succeeded in discovering any relation by which the constituents of Hume's bundles could be adequately held together. Some continuity of memory is necessary, but not, I think, sufficient. It needs to be backed by some other relation of which nothing more can be said but that it is the relation that holds between experiences when they are constituents of the same consciousness. The alternative is to regard it as a necessary proposition that a person's existence is tied to the existence of his body."[73] In this way for identity of a person "the two criteria of memory and bodily identity work together."[74] But now it may be objected that why should not the unity of a person's experiences, whether they are simultaneously or successive, be held to consist in their having a common relation to mental entity rather than various type of relations to one another? Ayer speaks of the relation of the sensible comprehence which holds relations between elements which are experienced together and the relation of sensible continuity which holds relations between elements which are felt to be continuous. It may be said that this implies the existence of a subject who has the experiences, in the sense that if something is felt, there must be something which feels it; if something is experienced, there must be something which experiences it, whether we call it a mind or a soul or anything else. This argument is plausible, but Ayer thinks it is fallacious. For he suggested, there is no reason why percepts should not be presented as spatio-temporally related, and no reason why temporal relations should not similarly hold between experiential data of different types."[75] About our possession of self-consciousness Ayer clearly says because we are able not only to be aware of our present feelings but also to be aware that we are aware of them and perhaps even aware that we are aware of them, and because of this prolonged indefinite sense there is a temptation to think of one's self, which is always a subject and never an object of consciousness. As in the system of Kant, there is a transcendental ego which stands outside this world. It is not in space and time and therefore not a possible object of experience. Being a radical empiricist Ayer cannot accept the existence of any such thing which has no empirical evidence. He argues, that "the self as such is not an object of acquaintance, not because it lies too deeply hidden but rather for a logical reason."[76] He says, "When Hume said that he could never perceive his self without one or more perceptions, or indeed perceive anything but the perceptions, he was not merely drawing attention to an empirical fact. Though this may not have been entirely clear to him, he had hit upon the logical point that nothing would count as one's discovering oneself apart from any perceptions."[77] According to Ayer, "What happens when one is self-conscious is that one claims some present or past experiences as one's own," and for one's self-identity, the occurence of experiences which are suitably related to one's body and to one another can be taken to be enough.[78]

In this way Ayer shows that the charge against empiricism that, it does not explain the connection between perception in virtue of which they formed a single self, is unfounded. For Ayer solves the problem of Hume by defining personal identity in terms of bodily identity, and bodily identity in terms of the resemblances and continuity of experience.

Now it may be argued that if Ayer rejects the idea of there being mental substances, then is he committed to denying the capacity of persons to exist apart from their bodies? Now-a-days this belief has been widely held that human being survive their corporal death, many of those who hold it they also hold that at some time their bodies will be restored to them, some others believe that their existence will be continued in a different body, it is also the belief of others that they will enjoy a misembodied existence. Ayer does not consider whether any of these beliefs has any good reason to hold. For the persons, who look forward to a "life after death," self is a metaphysical entity - the soul. And Ayer clearly says, "this metaphysical entity, concerning which no genuine hypothesis can be formulated, has no logical connection whatsoever with the self."[79]

Though Ayer defends the contention of Hume that to give a phenomenalist account of the nature of the self is necessary, but he clearly remarks that his actual definition of the self is not a mere restatement of Hume. For whereas Hume held that the self is the collection of sense experiences or the sense experiences which constitute a particular self are parts of it, Ayer holds that "The self is reducible to sense-experiences, in the sense that to say anything about the self is always to say something about the sense-experiences." And he says, "Our definition of personal identity is intended to show how this reduction could be made."[80]

V

In this way, to establish his own view of the self, Ayer examines other views concerning the problem of the self and shows the difficulties and mistakes contained in them. But the analysis of self proposed by Ayer itself is open to several objections. According to him all things, mental or physical' 'myself', 'otherselves', and physical bodies are nothing but logical constructions out of sense-experience. The questions are raised, who constructs this whole world? How is it possible to construct these things? Ayer has no satisfactory answer to these problems. Not only this, he fails to explain all basic problems of self like mind-body relation, self-consciousness, one's knowledge of other minds and personal identity.

In his venture to clarify the proposition of science and philosophy Ayer attempts to eliminate all metaphysical speculations with the help of a logical analysis of language, but in his enthusiasm for linguistic analysis he is inescapably committed to linguistic solipsism. Professor Harris in his Nature, Mind and Modern Science remarks that the view of logical empiricism "is confined to a solipsistic phenomenalism in which the knowing self, the objective world, and the minds of other persons are all spirited away in a mist of linguistic equivalence going by the name of logical construction, so that we are left only with a subjectless stream of sense-experience and a web of linguistic conventions, established and accepted by one cannot say whom; for minds are themselves but the product of logical construction, which is dependent on these very conventions, and thinking no more than the "behaviour" of yet other such logical constructions."[81] According to Professor Collingwood the final out come of empiricism is 'the uncharged' bankrupt of the modern philosophy.

Ayer's concept of the self-consciousness is also defective. In his view, all that is involved in self-consciousness is the ability of a self to remember some of its earlier states. But it would be clearly false to say that I am being conscious of myself as feeling and nothing is remembering my earlier states. Even if it is granted, the question is what is it that does remembering? On Ayer's account the self is a logical construction out of sense-content. But does a sense-content remember anything? Ayer's account fails to explain this problem. Similarly his explanation of the problem of personal identity is unsatisfactory. He defines personal identity in terms of bodily-identity, and solves the difficulty of uniting different bodily states of a person by the principle of spatio-temporal continuity. But this proposal of the principle of spatio-temporal continuity also fails to explain this unity. In Hume, Ayer finds it difficult to solve the problem of personal identity in terms of experience because there is no general principle for the unity of experience. Suresh Chandra remarks, "—— personal identity is also not definable in terms of bodily identity since there is no general principle for uniting different bodily states. To say that these bodily states are contingently related, or that they are found together, or they succeed one after another, with or without any spatio-temporal gap, is not at all to make any advance over Hume's difficulties."[82] And besides this principle of spatio-temporal continuity there is no other principle proposed by Ayer which may be found superior to this. For in his latest visiting The Central Questions of Philosophy, which was first published in 1973, he continues to speak of the principle of spatio-temporal continuity.[83]

Another difficulty in Ayer's account is, how different bodily states are ascribed to one and the same person. On Ayer's account mind is not a substance, but it is a series of experiences. The question is, what is that principle which is involved in bridging two different experiences into the same series? If it is said that because they are owned by one and the same person, it can not be, for this presupposes that they belong to the same series. The answer cannot be that they are owned by the same person because they are caused by one and the same body. For otherwise the difficulty will be about the expression 'the same body.' It also cannot be said that "because I locate my experiences in these bodily states, therefore, if the experiences are mine the bodily states are also mine. This answer would lead, first, to the psychological criterion of personal identity which has already been rejected by Ayer. Secondly, instead of the experiences being identified in terms of a body and its states, a body and its states would be identified in terms of experiences; and such an identification has already been prohibited by Ayer."[84] Here it is to be noted that Ayer himself accepts this defect in his account. "It may well be thought a defect in my position that it requires the existence of these psycho-physical relations to be assumed a-priori. But if this is a defect it is one that I see no way to remedy."[85] Ayer's account of the self is, thus, entirely unsatisfactory as it fails to solve all the basic problems of the self.

REFERENCES

1. Ayer, *Language, Truth and Logic*, p. 125.
2. *Ibid.*, p. 123.
3. Ayer, *Language, Truth and Logic*, p.123.
4. *Ibid.*, p. 123.
5. Ayer, *Language, Truth and Logic*, p. 124.
6. Ayer, *Language, Truth and Logic*, p. 124.
7. *Ibid.*, p. 125.
8. *The Problem of Knowledge*, p. 199.
9. *The Concept of a Person*, p. 52.
10. Ayer, *The Problem of Knowledge*, p. 199.
11. *Ibid.*, p. 201.
12. Ayer, *The Problem of Knowledge*, p. 202.
13. C.E.M. Joad, *A Critique of Logical Positivism*, pp. 102-103.
14. C.E.M. Joad, *A Critique of Logical Positivism*, p. 103.
15. L.S. Stebbing, *Logical Positivism and Analysis*. British Academy Annual Philosophical Lecture, 1933.
16. Ayer, *Language, Truth and Logic*, p. 128.

17. *Ibid.*, p. 130.
18. *Philosophical Essays*, pp. 191-192.
19. *Philosophical Essays*, pp. 193-194.
20. *Ibid.*, p. 194.
21. *Philosophical Essays*, pp. 201-202.
22. *Language, Truth and Logic*, p. 129.
23. *Philosophical Essays*, p. 202.
24. *Philosophical Essays*, p. 202.
25. *Ibid.*, p. 203.
26. *Philosophical Essays*, p. 204.
27. *Ibid.*, p. 204.
28. *Ibid.*, p. 204-205.
29. *Language, Truth and Logic*, p. 130.
30. *The Concept of a Person*, p. 82.
31. *Ibid.*, p. 82.
32. Vide, Descartes' *Discourse on Method*, Part V.
33. Ayer, *The Concept of a Person*, p. 83.
34. Ayer, *The Central Questions of Philosophy*, pp. 113-114.
35. Ayer, *The Central Questions of Philosophy*, p. 114.
36. *Ibid.*, p. 114.
37. *Ibid.*, pp. 114-115.
38. Ayer, *The Concept of a Person*, p. 83.
39. *Ibid.*, p. 83.
40. Ayer, *The Concept of a Person*, p. 83.
41. Ayer, *The Concept of a Person*, p. 84.
42. *Ibid.*, p. 84.
43. *Ibid.*, p. 84.

44. Ayer, *The Concept of a Person*, p. 85.
45. Ayer, *The Concept of a Person*, p. 86.
46. *Ibid.*, p. 87.
47. Ayer, *The Concept of a Person*, p. 86.
48. Strawson, *Individual*, p. 99.
49. *The Concept of a Person*, p. 87.
50. *Philosophical Investigations*, i, 293.
51. *The Concept of a Person*, pp. 87-88.
52. *The Concept of a Person*, pp. 104-105.
53. *Ibid.*, p. 105.
54. *The Concept of a Person*, pp. 105-106.
55. *Ibid.*, p. 106.
56. *The Concept of a Person*, p. 109.
57. *Ibid.*, p. 109.
58. *Ibid.*, p. 89.
59. *Ibid.*, pp. 115-116.
60. *Ibid.*, p. 116.
61. *The Concept of a Person*, p. 116.
62. Hampshire, *Thought and Action*, pp. 47-48.
63. *The Concept of a Person*, p. 93.
64. Hampshire, *Thought and Action*, p. 75.
65. *The Concept of a Person*, p. 112.
66. *Ibid.*, p. 112.
67. *Treatise of Human Nature*, Book I, Part IV, Sec. VI.
68. *Treatise of Human Nature*, Book I, Appendix.
69. Ayer, *The Origins of Pragmaticism*, p. 266.
70. *The Central Questions of Philosophy*, p. 115.

71. *The Central Questions of Philosophy*, pp. 115-116.

72. *Ibid.*, p. 116.

73. Ayer, *Problem of Knowledge*, pp. 198-199.

74. *Central Questions of Philosophy*, p. 116.

75. *The Central Questions of Philosophy*, p. 118.

76. *Ibid.*, p. 120.

77. *Ibid.*, p. 120.

78. *The Central Questions of Philosophy*, pp. 120-121.

79. Ayer, *Language, Truth and Logic*, p. 127.

80. *Language, Truth and Logic*, p. 128.

81. Harris, E.E., *Nature, Mind and Modern Science*, p. 351.

82. Suresh Chandra, *A Study in Ayer's Epistemology*, p. 204.

83. Ayer, *The Central Questions of Philosophy*, p. 118.

84. Suresh Chandra, *A Study in Ayer's Epistemology*, p. 205.

85. *The Concept of a Person*, p. 128.

6

A Critical Evaluation

I

William James divided all philosophical attitudes into two types and placed all the different doctrines of philosophy under either of the two categories. These two types of philosophical attitudes are, tough minded and tender-minded attitudes, which can alternately be called as worldly and other worldly types of thought. Realism, Empiricism, Naturalism, Positivism, Scepticism and Pragmatism are included under the category of tough-minded attitude and Speculative Metaphysics, Intuitionism, Rationalism, Idealism and various theological doctrines are included under the category of tender minded attitude. These attitudes are also characterised as attitudes of "Nothing But" and "Something More" respectively. In the twentieth century logical empiricism is the latest development of the tradition of empiricism in the history of western philosophical thought, and it has left a great impact on the philosophical thinking of contemporary times. An important characteristic of logical empiricism is the systematic pursuit of the problem of meaning by means of a logical analysis of language. It is specially in this respect that logical empiricism is distinguishable from the more psychologically oriented types of earlier empiricism. There are three important factors responsible for the growth and development of logical empiricism in contemporary philosophy. They are (1) the latest researches in logic and mathematics done by Russell, Hilbert and Brouwer etc., (2) a revolutionary revision of the basic concepts of physics caused by the works of Einstein, Planck, Bohr and Heisenberg and (3) the reforms brought about in the field of psychology by the researches of behaviourists like Pavio, Watson etc.

All these developments in the various fields of knowledge necessitated an inquiry into the limits and structure of a meaningful discourse. Through the discovery of logical and mathematical paradoxes, Russell made a mighty attempt to establish that traditional logic was to be revised in the light of his theory of types which resolved the paradoxes found in the traditional logical and mathematical concepts. Thus his theory of types had to be incorporated in logic in order to avoid the inconsistencies in the logical and mathematical thinking of the earlier type and it caused a revolution in the field of logical and mathematical researches. Einstein also caused revolution by his principle of relatively and by showing that the traditional concepts of absolute space and absolute time are devoid of meaning. Likewise the behaviourists tried hard to lay down the objective procedures for the study in the mental life. They attempted to formulate the mental concepts in terms of physical language and were successful, to a large extent, in proving that most of the mentalistic concepts based on the assumption of "something more" are devoid of any scientific content.

It is under such circumstances that the Vienna Circle was established around 1929 under the leadership of Moritz Schlick, which subsequently developed in the form of logical positivism. The movement of logical positivism had before it the dual programme of the demonstration of the meaninglessness of all metaphysics and consolidation of the results of different sciences by reducing them to a universal language. To achieve this aim the logical empiricists made use of a logical analysis of language for clarification of conceptual confusion due to which most of the metaphysical theories were caused and also to pave the way for clear thinking in the field of philosophy. Thus they made a full use of the technique of logical analysis to refute the rival theories of rationalism and idealism. They attempted to criticise all those logical foundations on which the rival theories were based. On this attempt their attitude is primarily negative, but they have also attempted to make a positive contribution to philosophy by way of providing explanations to such basic problems of philosophy as the nature of the external world and its objects, perception, mind and other minds, mind-body relation, recognition, memory and personal identity etc. As an exponent of logical empiricism Ayer attempts to solve all these problem of philosophy along the line of logical positivism.

II

Logical empiricists claim that philosophy is not a special type of study, i.e. speculative, but it is an analysis of words or sentences into genuine meaning. Philosophy is an inquiry into language. Though philosophers are not certain about the details of this programme, Ayer in his essay 'Philosophy and language,' which was delivered as an inaugural lecture at Oxford in November, 1960 and also published in The Concept of a Person, asserts "How this enquiry is to be conducted, what purposes it serves, how its progress is assessed, are questions which still need to be clarified ..... But however uncertain they may be about the details, there is now a fair measure of agreement among philosophers that theirs is what is technically called a second order subject. They do not set out to describe, or even to explain, the world, still less to change it. Their concern is only with the way in which we speak about the world. Philosophy it has been said, is talk about talk."[1] Thus logical empiricists identify philosophy with linguistic analysis. This concept of philosophy, in part, is a legacy of logical empiricism. The adherent of this movement are intended to purify philosophy of metaphysics and then to develop it as a branch of logic. They take interest in the language of science and assign that the function of philosophy is mainly to explicate terms which belong to scientific methodology. Thus in the movement of logical empiricism philosophy is seen as 'merging into science.' But the concept owes something to G.E. Moore and Ludwig Wittgenstein too. The view is influenced by Moore in the sense that he did assert that the function of analysis is not to discover some new facts but to clarify conceptual confusions. The business of a philosopher is to tell us what propositions mean. Though he denied that to conceive of philosophy as the practice of what he called analysis was necessarily to regard it as inquiry into language. For Moore, analysis was only one of the functions of philosophy. Philosophy was not a mere inquiry into language, but it was also concerned with facts for which linguistic expressions stood. The view is influenced by Ludwig Wittgenstein in rather different manner. He looked upon philosophical analysis as a form of intellectual therapy. He thought that people made mistakes by failing to understand the logic of our language. The failure to understand the logic of the language, gave rise to such problems which could not be easily resolved by philosophers and it created lot of confusions in philosophical thinking. The only remedy to overcome these difficulties was to trace-out the source of such confusions. This could be achieved only by a proper logical analysis of language.

The concept of philosophy that it is talk about talk owes something to Wittgenstein's thesis of intellectual therapy as it removes the misunderstanding of our language. But whereas Wittgenstein's thesis is only negative in form, the concept of linguistic analysis is not always negative. In its negative aspect it purifies philosophy of speculation but in its positive aspect it develops philosophy as a branch of logic. Thus regarding philosophy as talk about talk logical empiricists identify it with linguistic analysis. But the question is, can philosophy be identified with linguistic analysis? Kalidas Bhattacharya examines the view whether philosophy is linguistic analysis in his Philosophy, Logic and Language. He says, Philosophy is linguistic analysis may mean one of two things : (a) it is nothing but linguistic analysis and (b) it involves that analysis but is in itself something else. It should be noted that if philosophy is something more than analysis, the additional feature must come out of a critical consideration of analysis itself, not abextra, and those who hold that philosophy is nothing but linguistic analysis have not sufficiently analysed this linguistic analysis itself."[2] Philosophers who identify philosophy with linguistic analysis, claim that the only business of philosophy is linguistic analysis. Philosophy is sheer analysis of language, in both its semantic and syntactical aspect s."[3] In its semantic aspect philosophy analysis a complex word or sentence into simple reals, and in its syntactical aspect, it discovers the linguistic relations that cemented those reals into a complex concept. But this view is misleading. Language has, of course, an immense importance in the field of philosophical analysis. Philosophical analysis is made by thought, and thought involves language, but on this account they cannot be identified. Philosophy is concerned with the real. The real is not merely what a word or a sentence mean, it is also revealed by knowledge, which included non-sensuous intuition. Kalidas Bhattacharya argues "unless something is already known as real through any of the pramanas it cannot be meant by a word of sentence. If meaning has to be already known as real it follows that language is only a way of stating the real. It may state the real precisely or not precisely, precision being determined by the use of standard words and rules of syntax acceptable to the community to whom the expression is directed. From this point of view, language is secondary."[4] If philosophy is identified with analysis, if it is granted "only this secondary task of expressing what is known not only would this be undignified for philosophy, really there would be no task left for it, because every science and concrete discipline is under an equal obligation to express its points precisely."[5]

Ayer is a logical empiricist. According to the thesis of empiricism he asserts that philosophy interprets all propositions, except tautologies, in terms of sense-experience. Even granting this, there would arise a difficulty. If philosophy is to interpret all propositions in terms of sense-experience, then science is also under an equal obligation to do this. For the method of science is the method of observation, and observation is made by sensous experiences. And if it is so, there is no specific task left for philosophy. There would be no distinction between science and philosophy. Ayer distinguishes philosophy from sciences in such a way that their analysis are of different kinds. Philosophy does not analyse facts as of science but it analysis the meaning of fact. According to him, philosophy is concerned with the fact only with the way in which we speak about them. Now the difficulty is, "if there are only words and words and if the business of philosophy is only to reduce complex words or sentences to elemental words, one might still point out that the standard elemental words are relevant only to the community that uses them, and similarly with regard to the standard syntax. It would follow that meaning, and, therefore, philosophy itself, is relative and wholly conventional."[6] In any case philosophy cannot be identified with linguistic analysis. A philosopher analysis linguistic expressions, but it does not follow from this that philosophy is nothing more than linguistics. But, indeed through that it studies the reals which are expressed in linguistic expressions but known by knowledge including intuition. There is no doubt that linguistic analysis is a good tool to clarify confusions or to remove certain barriers in the way of philosophical thinking, but it is, after all, a means. Philosophy is not mere linguistic analysis. It cannot be reduced in linguistics or logic. It is different and more than this. Philosophy is an investigation of truth and values, it is concerned with reality. And linguistic analysis ignores this reality for which all philosophy is intended. Language is only an instrument of learning and expression. It has its own limitations, and in any investigation of truth and reality, one must realise its limitations.

III

To give a solid ground for their thesis, logical empiricists attempt to eliminate metaphysics. They give arguments against the possibility of metaphaysics and claim that the propositions of metaphysics are meaningless. They argue that language is constructed by the vocabulary and syntax. There are meaningful words and the rules of syntax which make a sentence meaningful. Metaphysical propositions are meaningless for they are either counter-semantical, in the sense that they contain words which are meaningless, or counter-syntactical in which words are meaningful but they are not in accordance with the rules of syntax. Such meaningless propositions are called "pseudo-propositions." They further argue that metaphysical propositions fail to conform to the conditions under which alone a sentence is literally meaningful. And, a sentence is literally meaningful, as Ayer writes, "if, and only if, the proposition it expressed was either analytic or empirically verifiable." Ayer concepts the Kantian distinction of analytic and synthetic (empirical) propositions, but he does not accept the definition of analyticity which was proposed by Kant. Analytic propositions, according to Ayer, are concerned with "relations of ideas." They are necessary and certain propositions for they are more tautologies. Analytic propositions are devoid of factual content. On the other hand, empirical propositions are concerned with 'matters of fact.' There are true of false empirical propositions. Empirical propositions are called synthetic propositions too. This distinction of analytic and empirical or synthetic propositions is open to several objections. By taking an example of analytic propositions 'either some ants are parasitic or none are' Ayer says, "It is independent of experience ..... provides no information whatsoever about the behaviour of ants or, indeed, about any matter of fact ..... is entirely devoid of factual content."[7] On the other hand he says, "the proposition there are ants which have established a system of slavery is a synthetic proposition. For we cannot tell whether or not it is true or false merely by considering the definitions of the symbols which constitute it. We have to resort to actual observation of ants."[8] The ground on which Ayer made this distinction is that empirical propositions are concerned with matters of fact whereas analytic propositions are devoid of factual content. The question is raised whether analytic propositions are wholly devoid of factual content? It is argued, "If the facts of experience are wholly missing then, what is the explanation of our usage of such term as 'ants,' 'parasitic,' etc.? If the proposition is completely devoid of factual content, then how could it have any terms the meaning of which depend on the facts of experience? If in a universe it is impossible to have such things as ants and their possibility of a universe having ants and their capacity to become parasitic, then one cannot claim that this proposition is completely devoid of factual content."[9] Kant made this distinction of analytic-synthetic proposition on the ground that whether a proposition extends the knowledge which we have or fails to extend it. A proposition is analytic for it fails to extend knowledge, but it does not follow from this that it gives no knowledge. Ayer disproves this Kantian distinction by pointing out that analytic prepositions are factually empty. Suresh Chandra discussed this problem of analitycity. In his view, a proposition can be factually empty in two different senses. It is factually empty, in the one sense, if its truth does not depend on the observation of facts. In the other sense, it is factually empty if it fails to give us any information about reality. In the Kantian sense, he writes, "these propositions are factually empty in the sense that their truth is independent of the observation of facts; but they are not factually empty in the sense that they give us no information about reality."[10] So to disprove this view Ayer has to prove not only that the proposition is factually empty in the one sense in which Kant proves but also in the other sense. But by taking the proposition as Ayer says, "one need not resort to observation to discover that there either are or are not ants which are parasitic." Suresh Chandra remarks that "Ayer has not given any argument to show that an analytic proposition is also factually empty in the other sense of the term. He has just taken it for granted that if a proposition is factually empty in the one sense of the term it is also factually empty in the other sense ... But .... one cannot simply assume it."[11]

Kant held that analytical judgements explain, synthetical judgements expand. In his view, "If in a judgement the predicate belongs to subject A as something that is already in a hidden manner contained in its concept, the judgement is called analytical. If B, though connected with the subject A, lies outside it, we speak of a synthetical judgement. ..... In an analytical judgement the predicate only discomposes or dissects the concept of the subject into partial concepts which are, confusedly, thought in it before. Synthetical judgements enrich or enlarge the concept of the subject by something now that could not be disengaged from it by any sort of dissection. Empirical judgements are all synthetical."[12] He further held, "For an analytical judgement I need no confirmation by experience. 'Every body has extention' is an analytical judgement, because I cannot think of a body without extension. 'Every body has weight' is a synthetical judgement founded on experience, for there might be bodies without weight, but when I say : 'Every thing that happens has a cause,' why do I regard to the notion of a cause as necessarily belonging to something that happens? On what does my mind rely when it connects these two conceptions? We feel that the connection is more general and necessary than experience alone can warrant. The connection must be entirely a priori. Synthetical judgements a-priori form the foundation of our whole theoretical knowledge."[13] Thus he comes on synthetic a-priori judgements and asserts that all theoretical sciences contain synthetic a-priori judgements as principles. A mathematical judgement like '7+5 = 12' is an a-priori judgement, not empirical, because it carries with it a necessity, which experience can never provide. But this is not an analytic proposition.

The concept of 12 is by no means already thought in merely thinking this union of 7 and 5; and I may analyse my concept of such a possible sum as long as I please, still I shall never find the 12 in it. We had to go outside these concepts, and call in the aid of the intuition which corresponds one of them. Arithmatical propositions are therefore always synthetic. This is still more evident if we take larger numbers. For it is then obvious that, however me might turn and twist our concepts, we could never, by the mere analysis of them, and without the aid of intuition, discover what (the number is that) is the sum."[14] Similarly he maintained that in metaphysics synthetic a-priori judgements are contained. "For" as he argued, "its business is not merely to analyse concepts which we make for overselves a-priori of things, and thereby to clarify them analytically, but to extend our a-priori knowledge. And for this purpose we must employ principles which add to the given concept something that was not contained in it, and through a-priori synthetic judgements venture out so far that experience is quite unable to follow us, as for instance, in the proposition, that the world must have a first beginning, and such like. Thus metaphysics consists of, at least in intention entirely a-priori synthetic propositions."[15]

Ayer rejects the possibility of synthetic a-priori propositions too. According to him Kant's criterion to make distinction between analytic and synthetic propositions is mistaken. "Kant does not give one straightforward criterion for distinguishing between analytic and synthetic propositions; he gives two distinct criteria, which are by no means equivalent. Thus his ground for holding that the propositions "7+5 = 12" is synthetic is that the subjective intension or "12"; whereas his ground for holding that "all bodies are extended" is an analytic proposition is that it rests on the principle of contradiction alone. That is, he employs a psychological criterion in the first of these examples, and a logical criterion in the second, and takes their equivalence for granted. But, in fact, a proposition which is synthetic according to the former criterion may very well be analytic according to the latter."[16] Thus he rejects the Kantian hypothesis that theoretical sciences contain synthetic a-priori propositions. For he argues, "while it is true that we have a-priori knowledge of necessary propositions, it is not true, as Kant supposed, that any of these necessary propositions are synthetic. They are without exception analytic propositions, or, in other words tautologies."[17] Here it is remarkable that though Ayer criticises Kant's explanation of analytic synthetic proposition and disproves synthetic a-priori proposition but he fails to explain even his position. Concerning the analytic proposition 'Oculist' is an eye doctor', Ayer says "it depends on the fact that the symbol 'eye doctor' is synonymous with 'Oculist'. And the same explanation holds good for every other a-priori truth."[18] He defines analyticity is terms of synonymity of symbols. But this definition has several difficulties. The objectionable feature of this definition is that it "is not general enough to cover all analytic propositions. It even fails to show the analyticity of those propositions which Ayer himself accepts as analytic. Ayer holds that the proposition 'Either some ants are parasitic or none are' is analytic, but this proposition does not possess a pair of synonymous symbols as does the proposition 'An oculist is an eye-doctor.'"[19] Another objection raised by Suresh Chandra is that "this definition leads to consequences which would be disliked by Ayer himself." He says, "Ayer has committed himself to the view that no analytic, i.e. a priori, proposition can be confuted in experience. And if he maintains that an analytic proposition cannot be confuted in experience because the symbols occuring in it are synonymous, then he should either accept that the propositions which do not have synonymous symbols are not analytic or he should accept the possibility of analytic propositions which could be confuted in experience. Either the proposition 'Either some ants are parasitic or none are' is not an analytic proposition at all for it does not have a pair of synonymous symbols - or it is analytic but could, possibly be confuted in experience."[20] It follows from this that Ayer has no clear conception why an analytic proposition cannot be confuted in experience. Ayer's position concerning the definition of analyticity is that no satisfactory explanation is obtained from him. His definition of analitycity is not acceptable as it fails to explain the analyticity of all analytic propositions.

In Ayer's view, a proposition is meaningful if it is either analytic or empiricially verifiable. Metaphysical propositions are claimed by him as meaningless, for they are neither analytic because they are not mere tautologies, nor empirically verifiable. But what then is the status of verification theory of meaning itself. The theory is commonly criticised by its opponents on the ground that the theory itself is not verified. Copleston finds it difficult to understand the status of the principle of verifiability that it is a proposition or no proposition. If it is a proposition, it should be, on Ayer's premises, either a tautology or an empirical hypothesis. It cannot be a tautology because from tautologies only further tautologies can be deduced. Neither it can be an empirical hypothesis for otherwise the principle is not a proposition it should, on Ayer's premises, be meaningless. Therefore he says, "In any case, if the meaning of an unexistential proposition consists, according to the principle, in its verifiability, it is impossible. I think to escape an infinite regress, since the verification will itself need verification, and so on indefinitely. If this is so, then all propositions, including scientific ones, are meaningless."[21] A.C. Ewing, in his article "Meaninglessness asserts that the verification theory of meaning itself is meaningless. According to him, "The statement that all meaningful statements are verifiable is not itself verifiable. It follows that if it is true it is meaningless."[22] Ayer may defend himself against such attacks by saying that it is note a statement but a proposal. Even then he cannot hope to get over the puzzle, for proposal itself requires verification. If Ayer claims metaphysical propositions as meaningless on the ground that they do not come in either category of meaningful propositions, they are neither analytic nor empiricially verifiable, then his own position is very much like that of a metaphysician, for the proposition which his own principle, or theory, or proposal expressed itself is neither analytic nor empirically verifiable. S. Radhakrishnan in his Philosophy - Eastern and Western, writes, "The view that problems of philosophy are linguistic is itself a hypothesis. The verification principle is a metaphysical statement, neither a tautology nor an empirical fact. It is a synthetic a-priori proposition of exactly the type that logical positivism intends to exclude. Logical positivism is itself a kind of metaphysics, a sceptical metaphysics."[23]

Copleston, in a debate with Ayer on Logical Positivism, which was held in 1949, asserts, "I have contended that metaphysical ideas has meaning if some experience is relevant to the formation of that ideas, and that a rational metaphysics is possible if there are, as I think there are, principles which express an intellectual apprehension of the nature of being. I think that one can have an intellectual experience on intuition if you like of being. A metaphysical proposition is testable by rational discussion, but not by purely empirical means. When you say that metaphysical propositions are meaningless because they are univerifiable in your sense, I do not think this amounts to more than saying that metaphysics are not the same thing as empirical science." He further says," ... logical positivism, apart from its theory of analytic propositions, simply embodies the notion of nineteenth century positivism that the terms "rational" and "scientific" have the same extention. This notion may correspond to a popular prejudice, but I see no adequate reason for accepting it."[24]

According to the theory of verification, verification of any statement must consist in one's having experiences of appropriate sort. But verification can occur only now and in future, how can one ever succeed in really meaning something about the past? In his later work Ayer himself accepts this difficulty, as he says, "—— it is no longer seems to me tenable —— if one came to doubt whether such or such an event did really occur, the only way in which one could hope to settle the question would by the discovery of further evidence. In practice, speculations about the past must relate to the traces which the past has left. Nevertheless the logical point remains that those traces are fallible. However, little reason one may have to distrust one's sources, their saying or indicating that such and such an event occurd does not logically entail that it did occur. And I think that this formal point needs to be respected, even when it has no practical application."[25] He feels that "Even in its weaker form, in which it is designed only to demarcate literal sense from non-sense, the verification principle runs into difficulties. .... The suggestion that a sentence is factually significant to a given person if, and only if, he knows that observations would lead him to accept or reject the proposition which it takes it to express, is not satisfactory, because it does not take account of the fact that people may behave irrationally."[26] Faced with the difficulties of verification theory Ayer shifts it to a rather different theory whereby "the meaning of a sentence is equated with the truth conditions of the propositions which it seems to express." This theory too cannot save the position of Ayer. For if it is said that the meaning of a sentence is equated with the truth conditions of the proposition which it serves to express, questions are raised what are the truth- conditions? How these truth conditions are established? If these truth conditions are established by some other truth-conditions than other truth conditions again requires further truth conditions, and it would be the fallacy of infinite regress. And this cannot be accepted by Ayer.

Ayer has attempted to refute not only the meaningfulness of the metaphysical propositions but also of the propositions of ethics, aesthetics and religion, because all such type of propositions are of the same type as the metaphysical propositions, that is, they are neither analytic nor empirically verifiable. Ayer agrees with Moore in maintaining that "good" is indefinable. But they differ from each other about the grounds on which "good" is declared as indefinable. For Moore's "good" is indefinable because it is a simple and unanalysable quality, but for Ayer, "good" is indefinable because it designates nothing at all. For Ayer, metaphysical propositions may be emotively significant, but they are devoid of any cognitive content. When we say that a certain type of action is right or wrong we do not make any factual statement. When we say that they are not factual statements we mean that the propositions which such statements express are neither true nor false. Thus all ethical propositions are declared as factually and cognitively devoid of meaning. All that such ethical propositions are intended to express is that there is something over and above the experience. But according to the logical empiricists all meaningful propositions consist of either analytic or empirical verifiable propositions and ethical statements are neither analytic nor empirical verifiable. At best ethics as a branch of knowledge can be nothing more than psychology and sociology. If we accept this position then we have to accept the empirical criterion of meaning, but such type of thinking involves the fallacy of "Petitio Principii." Logical positivists intend to prove that all ethical or metaphysical propositions are meaningless non-sense through their criterion of verifiability which is assumed without any justification of proof. The verification theory of meaning cannot claim any justification itself.

The criterion of verification itself has no logical validity because from the very beginning the logical empiricists assume that only the empirical propositions are meaningful and hence by implication they believe that all metaphysical propositions are meaningless. They unconsciously assumed that by meaning we are to understand the type of meaning the empirical statements have. From this Ayer infers that the factual statements alone have the kind of meaning which the criterion demands. That the factual statements alone have meaning "is something he is required to prove. But he assumes it. The empirical criterion of meaning, in fact, is not capable of demonstrating the impossibility of metaphysical propositions. Brand Blanshard advances some arguments against the emotive theory in his article The New Subjectivism in Ethics. By the new subjectivism in ethics he means the view that "when anyone says "this is right" or "this is good," he is only expressing his own feeling; he is not asserting anything true or false, because he is not asserting or judging at all; he is really making an exclamation that expresses a favourable feeling." He further mentions that "the view comes less from ethical analysis than from logical positivism."[27] One of the arguments of Blandshard against the view of the new subjectivism is about the notions of subjectively and objectively right. Moralists have made this distinction for many centuries. They maintain that there are some acts which would be the best acts to do in any situation; and these are the acts which are objectively right. On the other hand, sometimes we perform acts which we think that they are right, but we are mistaken; and then our acts are only subjectively right. Blandshard takes an example, and says, "A boy abuses his small brother. We should commonly say, "That is wrong, but perhaps he doesn't know any better. By reason of bad teaching and feeble imagination, he may see nothing wrong in what he is doing, and may even be proud of it. If so, his act may be subjectively right, though it is miles away from what is objectively right."[28] New subjectivism prohibits this distinction. According to this view, "If the boy feels this way about his act, when it is right in the only sense in which anything is right. The notion of an objective right lying beyond what he has discovered, and which he ought to seek and do is meaningless."[29] Now Blandshard argues, "if there is no such thing as an objectively right act, what becomes of the idea of duty? the idea of duty rests on the idea of such an act, since it is always our duty to find that act and do it if we can. But if whatever we feel approval for at the time is right, what is the point of doubting and searching further? Such a view seems to me to break the mainspring of duty, to destroy the motive for self-improvement, and to remove the ground for self-criticism."[30] Thus the propositions of values, of course, are not empirically verifiable, but on account of this they cannot be claimed as meaningless. Empirical verification is not the only criterion to judge the meaning of all statements. The verification principle of meaning cannot be applied to all forms of statements. According to Warnock, "It does not make sense to speak of the verification of commands, prayers, promises, expressions of intention, and so on; these accordingly do not fail to be verifiable; and to say of them that they cannot be verified is to make a somewhat trivial remark which in no way impugns their linguistic responsibility, and of course in no way implies that they are meaningless. The general conclusion, then, that non-satisfaction of the verification principle at once implied the verdict "meaningless" was always a foolish misunderstanding."[31] Moral and aesthetic experiences, spiritual realizations, introspection are higher human experiences, and they are so common to mankind. They are not sensous experiences, accordingly they are not verified empirically. But these higher experiences can also not be eliminated from the life of human beings. These human values are tested by reason. If one eliminates these values, he eliminates humanity itself. A man is a man due to his reason. A person is defined as a rational being. And if one eliminates rational values, man becomes of course, are not empirically verifiable, but on account of this they cannot be claimed as meaningless. Empirical verification is not the only criterion to judge the meaning of all statements. The verification principle of meaning cannot be applied to all forms of statements. According to Warnock, "It does not make sense to speak of the verification of commands, prayers, promises, expressions of intention, and so on; these accordingly do not fail to be verifiable; and to say of them that they cannot be verified is to make a somewhat trivial remark which in no way impugns their linguistic responsibility, and of course in no way implies that they are meaningless. The general conclusion, then, that non-satisfaction of the verification principle at once implied the verdict "meaningless" was always a foolish misunderstanding."[31] Moral and aesthetic experiences, spiritual realizations, introspection are higher human experiences, and they are so common to mankind. They are not sensous experiences and they are so common to mankind. They are not sensous experiences, accordingly they are not verified empirically. But these higher experiences can also not be eliminated from the life of human beings. These human values are tested by reason. If one eliminates these values, he eliminates itself. A man is a man due to his reason. A person is defined as a rational being. And if one eliminates rational values, man becomes nothing more than other animals. A person's life does not consist of mere sense-experiences which he derives from sense-organs. Human beings have certain aims, they have certain ideals of life by which their life-processes are guided. Ayer's view of logical empiricism fails to realize the basic truth of life, and consequently fails to grasp the values of morality, ethics and metaphysics.

IV

The problem of perception is also dealt by Ayer in accordance with his thesis of radical empiricism, William James in his collection of essays entitled The Meaning of Truth, explains this thesis. "Radical Empiricism," he says, "consists first of a postulate, next of a statement of fact, and finally of a generalized conclusion.

The postulate is that the only things that shall be debatable among philosophers shall be things definable in terms drawn from experience. (Things of an unexperienceable nature may exist ad libitum, but the form no part of the material for philosophic debate.)

'The statement of fact is that the relations between things, conjunctive as well as disjunctive, are just as much matters of direct particular experience, neither more not less so, than the things themselves.

The generalized conclusion is that therefore the parts of experience hold together from next to next by relations that are themselves parts of experience. The directly apprehended universe needs, in short, in its own right a concatenated or continuous structure."[32]

"What makes this a radical form of empiricism," Ayer says, is not the exclusion of anything which is not accessible to our experience but rather the refusal to differentiate between the objects of experience and its parts."[33] He further says," ..... experience has to be rich enough to furnish the entire world. Mind and matter, space and time, appearance and reality, all have to be constructed out of it."[34] Accordingly he explains his own view about perception.

A theory of perception requires the explanation of three elements - the perceiving subject, his act of perception, and the object of its act. Ayer explains the element of the perceiving subject not as a substantial self, mind or ego, but he explains it in terms of sense-experience as of Hume. According to him a perceiving subject, i.e. self or mind is a logical construction out of sense experience. To explain the second element of the act of perception Ayer accepts the view of indirect perception, according to which we do not perceive physical objects directly, but what we directly perceive is something else. In Ayer's view, sensedata are directly perceived. The third element, that is, the object of the act of perception is explained by Ayer as a logical construction out of sense-data. Thus in Ayer's philosophy both mind (the perceiving subject) and matter (the object of the act of perception) are explained according to his radical empiricistic view.

But Ayer fails to provide a satisfactory explanation of the theory of perception, as it involves many serious difficulties. The chief objections raised against his view are that he explains only one element of perception out of three, that is, the act of perception. The perceiving subject and the object of the act of perception are explained by him merely as logical constructions, which cannot be accepted. Not only this, even the element of the act of perception is defective. According to Ayer's view a thing is a logical construction out of sense-data. Here it is argued that "... sense-data are 'over and above' the physical objects, in the sense that it is out of them that a physical object is constructed. And the physical objects to which Ayer is referring are not verbal entities, they are what such words as 'tomatoes' and 'roses' etc., denote. But a non-verbal entity cannot be constructed out of verbal entities."[35] Suresh Chandra argues, "the sense-data which construct physical objects are non-verbal articles; they are what such words as 'colour-patches,' 'sounds,' and 'smells,' etc., denote. It is by bringing sense-data in this sense, that is, in a non-verbal sense, that the direct perception of a physical object was denied by Ayer. To perceive a physical object one has first to perceive sense-data. But this explanation is objectionable, for it clearly brings into existence the curious objects known as sense-data."[36] Professor Ryle in his The Concept of Mind remarks, this whole theory (of sense-data) rests upon a logical howler, the howler, namely of assimilating the concept of sensation to the concept of observation."[37] By calling it a howler he means that if observing something implies having a sensation then having a sensation cannot itself be a form of observation. For otherwise, in its turn it would involve having a further sensation, and in this way leading to an infinite regress. Perhaps Ayer would deny that his view has this disqualification. To avoid this type of objection Ayer interprets the terminology of sense-data in such a way that its introduction is not the introduction of a new class of entities. He maintains that in perceiving hands and tomatoes he has not to encounter some other items of the universe besides hands and tomatoes. The universe does not have two different classes of entities called physical objects as tomatoes and hands, and sense-data as colour patches, noises and smells. The terminology of sense-data, according to him, has nothing to do with this two-world theory. He says, "—— the purpose of making this distinction was simply to increase the utility and clarity of the sense-datum language by ensuring that its sentences should not be of the same logical form as those that refer to material things."[38] He explains that "two sentences may be said to have the same logical form if they can be correlated in such a way that to each expression that occures in either one of them there corresponds in the other an expression of the same logical type; and that two expressions may be said to be of the same logical type if any sentence that significantly contains either of them remains significant when the other is put in its place."[39] And he says, "it follows that if sentences referring to sense-data are of a different logical form from sentences referring to material things, it must not be assumed that precisely the same things can be said about them ..... But this does not rule out of the possibility that a proposition which is expressed by a sentence referring to a material thing can equally well be expressed by an entirely different set of sentences, which refer to sense-data; and this is what those who assert that material things are "logical construction" out of sense-data must be understood to claim."[40] Sometimes this view is put in the form of an assertion that "to say anything about a material thing is to say something, but not the same thing about classes of sense-data."[41] Ayer maintains that when he says that physical objects are constructed out of sense-data, he does not use the word "construction" in ordinary sense but in the sense of 'logical construction; And he elucidates the meaning of the expression 'logical construction' by the expressions of 'logical equivalence' and 'logical translation.' He maintains that by saying that a physical object is a logical construction out of sense-data, he simply means that statement about physical object is equivalent to the statement about sense-data, or that the statement about the physical object is translatable into the statement about sense-data. Still Ayer's view is not satisfactory. Suresh Chandra writes, "Ayer —— Ayer would try to avoid the difficulty by bringing some further difficulties - further difficulties in the sense that physical objects cannot be even logical construction out of sense-data, for a statement about a physical object is not logically equivalent to statements about sense-data. For no finite set of statements about sense-data is logically equivalent to a statement about a physical object; for if the members are infinite, then the set could simply not be formed. To say that something could be done by taking infinite steps is just a misleading way of saying that it could not be done."[42]

John Hospers in his An Introduction to Philosophical Analysis. Examines this phenomenalistic programme of translating physical object sentences into sense-datum sentence. According to Ayer, "—— what the statement that material things consist of sense-data must be understood to designate is not a factual but a linguistic relationship. What is being claimed is simply that the propositions which are ordinarily expressed by sentences which refer to material things could also be expressed by sentences which referred exclusively to sense-data."[43] In Hosper's view, "—— this too generates a problem. What are sense-datum statements about? Presumably they are about sense-data. But then sense-data are existents after all, and are to be included in the complete inventory of the universe." Yet Ayer denies that sense-data are objects like tomatoes and hands. According to him sense-data are about actual experience. But then "immediate experiences do occur and are to be included in the inventory of existents, along with physical objects."[44] Hospers further maintains, "there is much vacillation on this important point : sometimes sense-data are spoken of as if they were a separate class of existents, and sometimes as if they were merely ingredients in propositions, or "ways of talking." The vacillation is made all the more curious by the fact that writers speak as if they could stipulate what characteristic sense-data have; for example, "sense-data by definition have no properties other than those they appear to have." But if something exists, you don't stipulate its properties, you have to discover what they are."[45]

There are many other puzzles with sense-datum theory, like whether sense-data are mental or physical? If they are mental, physical objects cannot be constructed out of them; and if they are physical, mental objects like mind cannot be constructed; it is said that they are neither, but the raw material out of which both the mental and the physical objects are constructed, as the view of "neutral monism." Though we have already rejected this view that an object is a logical construction out of sense-data, but even granting this the question is raised, do they occur in space? It is said that they do not occur in physical space but in phenomenal space. Phenomenal space is constructed out of physical space. Space means "the aggregate of all our possible sensations."[46] Granted, but do they occur in time? Is there physical time or phenomenal time out of which physical time is constructed, as it is said in the case of space? It may be said that space is capable of being constructed out of sense-data which are directly given to us in sense-experience. Temporal duration like spatial extension is a relation between sense-data.[47] H.F.B. Winston in his article Myth of Sense-data asserts, "How do we determine the duration of sense-datum? If I blink my eyes while looking at a red patch, are there two sense-data separated in time, or is there only one interrupted in its career? If a change occurs in my visual field, has the sensedatum changed or been replaced by another? If the later, is there any reason why, when no change is observed, a sense-datum should not be replaced by another exactly like it? It may be said that to answer these questions is not important. I am inclined to agree that it is not; but the only reason I can see for this is that, sense-data being wholly fictitious entities, we can attribute to them what qualities we please."[48] There are many puzzles with the terminology of sense-data. Puzzles are followed by puzzles, and there is no apparent way to resolve them. From this it is maintained that sensedata are nuisance, sense-data do not exist at all, they are a myth, and the introduction of sense-data does not serve any useful purpose.

According to John Hospers, "Sense-datum philosophers have argued as follows:

1. I see a coin.
2. The coin is round.
3. The coin appears ellipical to me.

Therefore

4. I see an elliplical sense-datum.

But (so runs the criticism) this argument is fallacious. That the coin appears elliptical to me is no reason whatever for concluding that there is anything (a sense-datum) there is elliptical, it is the coin that is round and appears ellipitical. We don't need a sense-datum in the picture at all. There are no sense-data to appear : physical objects appear, and they have varying appearances depending on varying condition of perception. This at any rate is the thesis of the theory of appearing physical objects appear and their appearances are various. But there is no such thing as a sense-datum that is the apperance."[49] The theory of appearing, i.e. physical objects appear and their various appearances may be applied to the case of differential certainty like figure in a marble museum is mistaken for a real woman, or in the case of perceptual relativity like from a distance a large tower looks small or green hills look purple or from an angle the round coin looks elliptical. But the question is how this theory is applied to the case of total hallucination? What is it that appears where there is no physical thing at all like the drunkard sees pink rats where there are no pink rats, or Macbeth sees a dagger where there is no dagger? According to F.H.B. Winston, "It is misleading —— to say that there exists "A dagger like appearance," though we need not be misled by such a use of the word "appearance" if we are careful. Strictly speaking, however, there are no such things as appearances. To suppose that there are, would be like supposing that Mr. X put in an appearance, but there must have been something over and above Mr. X which he was kind enough to put in. "Mr. X appeared," that is the proper mode of expression if we are to avoid difficulties."[50] John Hospers' comment on this point is that "whether this kind of reasoning is satisfactory has been disputed. It is true that there is nothing over and above Mr. X, for Mr. X himself appears here there is something to do the appearing. But when there is no physical object at all, what does the appearing? It would seem that there is nothing at all, and that therefore the analogy between the situation of Mr. X and the hallucination does not hold. What, then, are we to do? Perhaps we must resort to sense-data again or, if this term is too theory-laden as immersed in invalid distinctions, we must resort to something we admittedly do have, and that is sense-experiences. And so the dispute continues."[51]

The Ayer's account of the theory of perception is open to several difficulties. It fails to explain any of the three elements which a satisfactory theory of perception is required to do.

Neither could it explain the perceiving subject, nor the object of the perception, nor even the act of perception. And it is for this reason that this sense-datum theory of perception is claimed by some philosophers as a nuisance. It does not serve any useful purpose to the theory, but only raises some more difficulties.

V

Ayer analyses the notion of 'self', as it is already maintained, in accordance with his thesis of radical empiricism. He rejects the possibility of self as a metaphysical entity. In his view, self is a logical construction out of sense experience. And a sense-experience is a whole composed of sense-contents. Sense-contents are parts of a sense-experience, but they are elements of a logical construction. According to him, one cannot significantly speak of a sense-experience or of a sense-content as a logical construction out of sense-contents. First, difficulties are raised with the term 'logical construction.' It is argued that Ayer's argument could not show that an experience or a sense-content cannot be a logical construction. The notion of logical construction is applicable to a sense-content and to a sense-experience. Suresh Chandra writes "taking the case of a sense-content, one cannot say in connection with it that its being an element of a logical construction excludes the possibility of its being itself a logical construction, there are logical constructions the elements of which are themselves logical constructions."[52] If it is said that logical construction is complex, for it can be analysed further, and sense-contents are simple, for it cannot be 'analysed' further. And to be a logical construction sense-contents are required to be complex which they are not. But then it is argued " —— a sense experience is complex because it is a whole 'composed of a sense-contents.' It is difficult to find a good ground for denying a sense-experience to be a logical construction."[53] May be that Ayer denied sense-experience as a logical construction to avoid the duplication of logical construction in his explanation of self. For an inquiry into the nature of a self seems to be limited to one logical construction and its constituents, or in other words a self and what constitutes it. And if sense- experiences are also described as logical constructions then an inquiry into the nature of a self would extend, at least, to two logical constructions which would be an unnecessary complication. Ayer may assert that he refrains from describing sense-experiences as logical constructions because he wanted to avoid the act-object analysis of sense-experience. For if he defines sense-contents as the object of sense-experience then he must accept the legitimacy of act-object relation, which according to him, cannot be legitimate. But, then, it is argued that "the act-object relation is ruled out even in the condition in which a sense-experience is made a logical construction out of sense-contents. For example, though a table is a logical construction out of certain sense-contents, it does not imply that the table is an act and the sense-contents involved are the objects of such an act. The statement that a table is a logical construction simply means that there is no table over and above its sense-contents." "Though," it is remarked that "it may be wrong to describe a sense-experience as a logical construction, such a description cannot be prohibited simply on the ground of avoiding the act-object analysis."[54]

Even granted that self is a logical construction out of sense-experiences, the question is raised how is the self distinguished from the not self or how is a person distinguished from a physical object? In Ayer's opinion the distinction between the self and the not-self or mind and matter is of secondary importance. There is no fundamental distinction between them in the sense that they both are logical constructions. One logical construction is distinguished from another on the basis that they are 'constituted by different sense-contents or sense-contents differently related.' Concerning the nature of sense-contents, Ayer adopts the view of 'neutral monism' and holds that sense-data are neither mental nor physical; they are raw material out of which both mental and physical objects are constructed. The distinction of mind and matter applies only to logical constructions. In this way the distinction between the self and the not-self is merely a distinction in the sense-contents involved and the relations between these sense-contents. But it is argued that it is not the case. Suresh Chandra asserts, "From what Ayer says it follows that a self is a logical construction in a sense quite different from that in which a book is a logical construction. A self is a logical construction out of sense-experiences, whereas a book and a table are logical construction out of sense contents. A sense content does not mean the same thing as a sense-experience. A sense-content is a part of a sense-experience. The sense in which it is a part implies that a sense experience is a whole. And if a whole is different from its parts, then a sense-experience must be different from a sense content. And if this difference is granted, then to say that a self is a logical construction out of sense-experiences cannot mean the same thing as to say that it is logical construction out of sense-contents."[55] Not only this, he goes on and remarks that though Ayer says that the self is a logical construction but he himself makes statements from which it can be inferred that it is not a logical construction at all. Ayer denies that a sense experience is a logical construction and that a sense content is an element of a sense-experience. This clearly implies that the self is not ultimately analysable in terms of sense-contents and a statement about the self is not translatable in terms of statements about sense contents. So the self cannot be a logical construction at all, if it is implied that in the definition of a logical construction that it is ultimately analysable in terms of sense-contents and a statement concerning it is ultimately translatable in terms of statements concerning sense-contents." He continues, "if it cannot be a logical construction then the question of considering it as a logical construction out of sense-experiences also does not arise."[56] Several other mistakes are found in his explanation of the self. One of the serious mistakes is in his concept of the separateness of bodies. For if he maintains that all the sentences referring to body are translatable into sentences referring to sense-contents, and similarly sentences referring to mind are translatable into sentences referring to sense-contents, then the distinction in its application to mind and to body can legitimately be described as pseudo. And if this distinction is pseudo, then Ayer's assertion that it is not impossible for a sense-content to be an element of a mental and physical object, cannot deny the possibility that it may be an element of two physical objects. Whereas he asserts that it is logically impossible for any sense-content to be an element of more than one body. And if it is possible for any sense-content to be an element of more than one body, the concept of the separateness of bodies, and also the concept of the separateness of selves for it is derived from separateness of bodies, would break down.

Ayer's analysis of the concept of self-consciousness is also unsatsifactory. Like Hume, Ayer explains the nature of self-consciousness with the help of the principle of memory. He says, "For all that is involved in self-consciousness is the ability of the self to remember some of its earlier states."[57] But this view is objectionable. According to an empiricist's explanation 'I am conscious of myself' means I am conscious of my experience.' Now, if the self-consciousness is the ability of a self to remember some of its earlier states, or if self-consciousness is the ability of memory, then in saying that 'I am conscious of my experience' would simply mean that 'I am conscious of my past experience,' or that 'I am conscious now that there is a pen in my hand' would suggest that I am conscious of my past experience, and this is absured to suggest. Memory involves merely one's consciousness of past experience. But if one is conscious of one's present experience, then the analysis of self-consciousness in terms of memory or in terms of the ability of a self to remember some of its earlier states, is wrong. In his later work The Concept of a Person, Ayer analyses the concept of consciousness as thinking about a problem, or remembering some events, or seeing or hearing something, or deciding something, or feeling some emotions, entails being conscious. But this analysis of self-consciousness is also defective. It is a false interpretation of self-consciousness. For if it is so, then what is it that which does thinking, or remembering, or feeling? Ayer analyses self as a logical construction out of sense-experience. And a self-consciousness is a consciousness of self. Then is it the ability of sense-contents to think or to remember or to hear or to see something? Ayer, like other logical empiricists, fails to give a satisfactory answer to such questions. J.P. Shukla writes "In their enthusiasm for the clarification of the terminology of science and philosophy by demolishing all metaphysical speculations through linguistic analysis, and logical positivists are inescapably committed to linguistic solipism."[58] if Ayer's analysis of the self is granted, then most of the objections that are raised against Hume's analysis of the self and that Ayer himself raised against Hume, are also applicable to Ayer's own analysis of the self. The fundamental objections against such a thesis are, to avoid the charge of solipsism to which such a thesis is open, to bring unity to different experiences of a person, and to identify these experiences, i.e. to explain the problem of personal identity.

As regards the objection of solipsism, if one defines self in terms of sense-experiences, and experiences are characterised as private or subjective, then it is logically impossible for one person to have the experiences of another. And if one has no access to the experiences of others, then there is no logical ground for him to believe in the existence of others. To defend himself against this objection, Ayer maintains that the objection of solipsism contradicts the basic assumption of his analysis. For his analysis of the self is not restricted to oneself but it is applicable to the other selves too. Here it is argued solipsism may be false or absurd, but that is a different question. The rejection of solipsism follows from the very definition of philosophy as analysis of meaning. For the function of such a philosophy is not to establish the meaning or truth of a proposition used in a natural or artificial language, but to give analysis of its meaning. Since solipsism implies that such propositions as 'he is in pain' and 'He is happy' are senseless therefore it cannot be accepted as a legitimate analysis of the self. Solipsism cannot imply that these propositions are false; for if they are false there is a possibility of other persons to exist. So these propositions have to be senseless if solipsism is true. So the difficulty before Ayer is to avoid the solipsistic consequence from his analysis."[59]

Ayer may avoid this solipsistic consequence by accepting the argument from analogy for the existence of other person. But he does not accept the validity of the argument from analogy. He asserts that it is logically impossible for the experiences of others to occur in my sense-history, and it follows from this that the argument from analogy cannot be applicable with regard to the existence of these experiences. Another way to establish the experiences of other persons may be to publicise sense-experiences, because the puzzle is in accepting sense-experiences as private of subjective. And the way to publicise sense-experiences is that to accept that a sense-content could be an element of more than one body. And if sense-experiences are publicized it would be possible for one to have numerically the same experiences which others are having. But Ayer does not accept this way to publicise sense-experience too for avoiding the solipistic consequence from his analysis. He tries to abolish the subjectivity of experiences by a behaviouristic interpretation of them. To give a behaviouristic interpretation of the experiences of others, he is logically led to give the same interpretation to his own experiences because the concept of experience is applicable to oneself as well as to others. According to Ayer, experiences are private but they are expressed in the bodily behaviour. Thus he interprets the experiences or others as well as one's own in terms of their bodily expressions or bodily behaviour. He says, "Just as I must define material things and my own self in terms of their empirical manifestations, so I must define other people in terms of their empirical manifestations that is in terms of the behaviour of their bodies, and ultimately in terms of sense-contents."[60]

Ayer does not stop at bodily behaviour, he goes on and reduces bodily behaviour to sense-content. And this reduction of the sense-contents is extended to the bodily identity. Now the question arises whether or not the interpretation of the experiences of others or the existence of other person in terms of bodily behaviour is legitimate. The answer is, it is not. Ayer's proposal to reduce the experiences of persons to their bodily behaviour leads to difficulties. If the bodily behaviour of other persons is defined in terms of sense-contents. The question is, what kind of sense-contents are supposed to be considered for this purpose? If it is said that these sense-contents are private in terms of which the bodies of other persons are defined, then the inter-subjective observability of these bodies would be given up. And a body would become a private property as well as sense-experiences of a person. But if bodies are intersubjectively observable then they must be defined in terms of public sense-contents. And the concept of public sense-contents is self-contradictory, as Ayer maintains that it is logically impossible for a sense-content to be a part of two different sense-experiences belonging to two different sense-histories. It follows from this that "it is also not possible to have an intersubjectively observable body, for the concept of intersubjectively observable body becomes itself a self-contradictory concept. This further implies that the substitution of bodily behaviour for sense-experiences is philosophically pointless.[61]

Ayer defines personal identity in terms of bodily identity. He refers to the body as the owner of experiences. As he says, "The experiences which might then ensure may themselves be imaginable; but it would seen that increditing them with an owner we are making a tacit reference to the body which is supposed to have been forsaken."[62] In saying 'a person is a owner of experience' is nothing more than a body is a owner of experience. So a person is not defined in terms of mind, or mind and body, but only in terms of a body. He further remarks that "a person's ownership of states of consciousness consists in their standing in a special causal relation to the body by which he is identified."[63] In this way a person owns certain experiences simply means that certain experiences stand in a causal relation to his body. And from this it implies that the relation of ownership is a metaphorical expression for the causal relation. To adopt this view of a person and personal identity as a bodily identity, Ayer tries to avoid the difficulties of empiricism which he himself feels that Hume's view was open. Referring to Hume's concept of the self, Ayer writes, "if it is regarded as a collection of experiences, there is the problem, to which Hume himself confessed that he could see no answer, of showing how the collection is united with any view of this type, there is also the problem of identifying the experiences themselves. In the ordinary way, we identify experiences in terms of the person whose experiences they are; but clearly this will lead to a vicious circle if persons themselves are to be analysed in terms of their experiences."[64] This remark implies that he finds two difficulties in Hume's concept. The first is that it could not unite different experiences of a person and the second is that Hume's concept could not identify these experiences. But Ayer's view of the self, too, does not remove any difficulty of modern empiricism. As regards the difficulty of uniting different experiences of a person Ayer's view itself requires this unity. Ayer defines personal identity in terms of bodily identity, but it also involves the difficulty of uniting different bodily status of a person. Ayer proposes the principle of spatio-temporal continuity to avoid this difficulty. As he says, "the criteria for the identity of persons will be the same as those that determine the identity of their bodies and these will confirm to the general conditions which govern the identity of all physical objects of a solid macroscopic kind. It is primarily a matter of spatio-temporal continuity."[65] But if this view is rejected that personal identity is defined in terms of experiences on the ground that there is no general principle for the unity of experiences, on the same ground this view is also rejected that personal identity is defined in terms of bodily identity, for there is no general principle for uniting different bodily states. Ayer does not make any advance over the difficulty of Hume by suggesting that these bodily states are contingently related, or they succeed one after another, with or without any spatio-temporal gap. For the main question how different bodily states are united to one and the same person still remains unsolved.

Ayer's view of the self fails to explain all the problems, regarding the nature of self, and is enmeshed in several serious difficulties and insurmountable paradoxes. Ayer analyses the whole world in terms of a logical construction. According to Weinberg "all this is a logical construction within 'one experience' and that sentences used by other persons are never symbols but only fact instances of behaviour."[66] But, as J.P. Shukla writes, if 'myself' as well as 'other selves' and material bodies are the constructions out of the total mass of elementary experience, how this constructing is possible? Who constructs this world? The logical positivists fail to furnish a satisfactory account of the problem of the 'how' and the 'why' of the construction."[67] Though Ayer and other logical empiricists attempt to demolish all metaphysical speculations by the logical analysis of language and yet in doing so they have to presuppose the existence of a mind because all logic presupposes a mind which does the logical thinking and declares arguments to be valid and invalid and propositions to be true or false on the basis of some objective criteria of meaningfulness.

VI

Every new idea, theory and movement plays an important role in the development of philosophical thought and makes a contribution to the total fund of knowledge. Logical positivism, as a philosophical movement, has also done the same in the development of philosophy in the twentieth century. And as no view is perfect likewise logical positivism suffers from certain defects and has its own limitations. A study, analysis and evaluation of Ayer, who is a typical representative of the movement of logical positivism, gives us an opportunity to assess the merits and demerits of his philosophy in particular and logical positivism in general. Ayer devotes all his works to justify, elaborate and defend the central theme of logical positivism which was initiated by the Vienna Circle under the leadership of Moritz Schlick around 1929.

In pursuance of the programme of the logical positivists, Ayer attempts to eliminate metaphysical propositions with the help of logical analysis of language. In this context, he lays great emphasis on the principle of verification. The principle of verification may be important from the point of view of an empirical investigation of the world of facts, but it cannot be accepted as the principle having universal application to all the spheres of human experience. During the course of the discussion of this principle in the context of the knowledge of the past and of other minds, Ayer himself admitted its limitations and modified this principle as verification in the weak sense and also admitted that when we speak of verification even in the weak sense we have to be satisfied only if it is only theoretically verifiable. Not only this, the principle suffers from certain logical difficulties which have been pointed out by different philosophers. Even if we accept the validity of the principle of verification, it may have justification for the empirical world, but it does not mean that it can undo all metaphysical thinking.

In order to prove the thesis of logical empiricism, Ayer, like all other logical positivists and empiricists, has to give an explanation of the a-priori in consistency with his theory of radical empiricism. Even on this point Ayer does not seem to have made a substantial advance on the distinction of the synthetic and the analytic propositions made by Kant. The traditional philosophers and logicians also believed that all analytic propositions are formal. The only point which Ayer tribes to prove is that there is no possibility of and justification for the synthetic a-priori propositions. But as we have seen, during the discussion of the problem, that Ayer's attempt to refute the possibility of synthetic a-priori propositions is not entirely justified. Many critics have pointed out that Ayer's principle of verification itself is a case of the type of synthetic a-priori propositions which he attempts to refute.

When Ayer deals with the problem of perception and the nature of the external world, he, in consistency with the doctrine of the empiricism, tries to explain everything in terms of sense-data. The term sense-datum is introduced by some contemporary philosophers in order to explain certain problems of perceptual knowledge like illusion and hallucination etc. In fact the term sensedata reminds us of the term ideas as used by the older empiricists with a substantical distinction that whereas ideas have a psychological content, sense-data seem to be neutral in this respect. But as the great amount of discussions about the nature of sense-data by such contemporary philosophers as Moore, Russell, Price, Broad etc., and the divergent view expressed by them reveal that the theory of sense-data is an engima to the contemporary empiricists. Ayer holds that all physical objects and mind are nothing but logical constructions out of sense-data. On this point he does not seem to make any substantical advance on Russell's theory of 'Neutral monism.'

Another important problem for Ayer was that of the mind and its relation to body and other minds. In this connection Ayer has to solve such difficult problems like recognition, memory, personal identity etc. The reality of mind is such a glaring fact that it seeks a satisfactory explanation from every satisfactory theory of philosophy. In his Language, Truth and Logic, Ayer's explanation of the nature of mind is very much like that of David Hume. But when he was confronted with certain difficulties, he modified his position in his later writings. While dealing with the problem of mind, Ayer fails to give a satisfactory explanation of such basic problems as personal identity and self-consciousness. His attempt to explain personal identity in terms of bodily identity reverts his position to a sort of materialism, which is not explicitly accepted by him. And any materialistic explanation of the problem of personal-identity cannot be taken to be a satisfactory one. When Ayer comes to the problem of self-consciousness, he utterly fails in giving a satisfactory explanation of it. If mind is a logical construction out of sense-data, the question arises whether consciousness is an adventitious quality which suddenly arises at some stage or the other during the logical construction of mind of sense-data or is it an essential quality of sense-data. Like all other logical positivists and empiricists. Ayer is not clear on this point and he fails to speak with confidence in respect of some such problems. What is more important is that as a logical positivist, Ayer could have taken some help from contemporary theories of psychology in this field, because the growth of positivism largely depends upon the growth and development of empirical sciences by which the movement of logical empiricism is deeply influenced. Even if we study some modern psychological theories in respect of certain problems of mind, we observe that their findings reveal that there are realms of human mind which are not limited to the spheres of ordinary human experience. I am deliberately pointing out this fact because in some of his works, a mention of which has already been made in the present work, Ayer deals with the problems of para-psychology in a half-hearted fashion. All this reveals that Ayer's theory of mind is not at all satisfactory.

Another important theme of the logical positivists is that of the emotive theory of ethics. Following the tradition of the logical positivism Ayer supports the emotive theory of ethics and asserts that all ethical, aesthetic and religious statements are devoid of any cognitive content. Thus entire ethics is reduced to the question of approval and disapproval, liking and disliking and preference and non-preference. The logical positivists had to adopt this view in order to have a consistent theory of empiricism because if they accept the ethical truth as something trans-empirical, such an acceptance goes beyond any consistent theory of empiricism. When we deal with the ethical problems, both in the case of individual as well as society, we cannot keep our perspective limited to questions of linking and disliking alone, because the conduct, decisions and actions of both the individual and society are evaluated on the basis of some objective principles. The emotive theory of ethics leads us not only to ethical relativism but also subjectivism and all subjectivism goes against the modern scientific temperament by which the attitudes of the logical positivists are enormously guided.

Thus a critical evaluation of Ayer's philosophy shows that his attempt to solve the central problems of philosophy is consistency with the doctrine of radical empiricism is not entirely satisfactory. However, Ayer has definitely been successful in bringing clarity to certain problems of philosophy by way of their analysis. Even if it is accepted that the role of philosophy is not that of science of all sciences or that it true function is not that of construction of metaphysical systems, the dignity and glory of philosophy is in no way minimised. Ayer's philosophy is a case to prove the truth that philosophy shall remain important and capture the attention of all serious thinking individuals as well as intellectuals with a new charm even if its function is only analysis of the basic problems of knowledge and truth. But, at the same time, it can not be denied that the true "aim of philosophy must be to probe into the nature of man and the world for the sake of understanding the nature of reality and the ordering of life in the light of one's understanding of the nature of reality. Analysis no doubt, is necessary. But it need not and should not be restricted in a narrow way to language alone. Just as it is necessary to analyse and examine the conceptual equipment and the linguistic expressions which we use with a view to clearing up the philosophical muddles and paradoxes arising as a result of the faulty use of language, it is equally necessary to analyse our experience as well as our existence in its varied forms. It is here that we find the breakdown of contemporary philosophy, since it is seriously concerned with the clarificatory function in respect of the language that we use, without being concerned with the meaning of the universe, or a unified conceptual scheme of the universe."[68]

REFERENCES

1. Ayer, *The Concept of a Person*, p. 3.
2. Kalidas Bhattacharya, *Philosophy, Logic and Language*, p. 1.
3. *Ibid*., p. 3.
4. Kalidas Bhattacharya, *Philosophy, Logic and Language*, p. 11.
5. *Ibid*., p. 12.
6. Kalidas Bhattacharya, *Philosophy, Logic and Language*, p. 13.
7. Ayer, *Language, Truth and Logic*, p. 79.
8. *Ibid*., pp. 78-79.
9. Suresh Chandra, *A Study in Ayer's Epistemology*, pp. 22-23.
10. *Ibid*., p. 25.
11. Suresh Chandra, *A Study in Ayer's Epistemology*, p. 25.
12. Rabel, Kant, p. 106.

13. Rabel, Kant, pp. 106-107.
14. Smith, Kant, *Critique of Pure Reason*, p. 33.
15. *Ibid.*, p. 34.
16. Ayer, *Language, Truth and Logic*, p. 78.
17. *Ibid.*, p. 84.
18. Ayer, *Language, Truth and Logic*, p. 85.
19. Suresh Chandra, *A Study in Ayer's Epistemology*, p. 34.
20. Suresh Chandra, *A Study in Ayer's Epistemology, p.* 34.
21. Edward and Pap, *A Modern Introduction to Philosophy* (Ed.), p. 618.
22. A.C. Ewing, *Meaninglessness, Mind*, 1937.
23. S. Radhakrishnan, *Philosophy—Eastern and Western*, Vol. II, p. 442.
24. A.J. Ayer and Father Copleston, Logical Positivism a debate, appeared in Edward and Pap's *Modern Introduction to Philosophy*, pp. 617-618.
25. Ayer, *The Central Questions of Philosophy*, p. 26.
26. *Ibid.*, pp. 25-26.
27. Edwards and Pap, *A Modern Introduction to Philosophy* (ed.), p. 434.
28. Edwards and Pap, *A Modern Introduction to Philosophy* (ed.), pp. 439-440.
29. *Ibid.*, p. 440.
30. *Ibid.*, p. 441.
31. Warnock, *English Philosophy Since 1900*, p. 46.
32. William James, *The Meaning of Truth*, pp. 11-13.
33. Ayer, *The Origins of Pragmaticism*, p. 225.
34. *Ibid.*, pp. 225-226.
35. Suresh Chandra, *A Study in Ayer's Epistemology*, p. 59.

36. Suresh Chandra, *A Study in Ayer's Epistemology*, pp. 59-60.
37. Gilbert Ryle, *The Concept of Mind*, p. 213.
38. Ayer, *The Foundations of Empirical Knowledge*, pp. 232-233.
39. *Ibid.*, p. 233.
40. Ayer, *The Foundation of Empirical Knowledge*, p. 233.
41. Vide A.E. Duncan-Jones, "Does Philosophy Analyse Common Sense?" Aristotelian Society Supplementary Proceedings, 1937, pp. 140-141.
42. Suresh Chandra, *A Study in Ayer's Epistemology*, p. 60.
43. Ayer, *Foundations of Empirical Knowledge*, p. 232.
44. John Hospers, *An Introduction to Philosophical Analysis*, p. 559.
45. *Ibid.*, p. 559.
46. Ayer, *The Origins of Pragmatism*, p. 234.
47. *Ibid.*, p. 244.
48. Winston H.F. Barnes, "The Myth of Sense-Data", proceeding of the Aristotelian Society, XLV (1944-45) 100. The authors term "sensum" has been replaced by the word "sense-datum" to preserve consistency of terminology.
49. John Hospers, *An Introduction to Philosophical Analysis*, pp. 561-562.
50. Winston F.H. Baranes, *op. cit.*, pp. 113-114.
51. Hospers, John, *An Introduction to Philosophical Analysis*, p. 563.
52. Suresh Chandra, *A Study in Ayer's Epistemology*, p. 132.
53. *Ibid.*, p. 133.
54. Suresh Chandra, *A Study in Ayer's Epistemology*, p. 133.
55. Suresh Chandra, *A Study in Ayer's Epistemology*, p. 135.
56. Suresh Chandra, *A Study in Ayer's Epistemology*, pp. 137-138.
57. Ayer, *Language, Truth and Logic*, p. 126.
58. J.P. Shukla, *The Nature of Mind*, p. 105.

59. Suresh Chandra, *A Study in Ayer's Epistemology*, pp. 148-149.
60. Ayer, *Language, Truth and Logic*, p. 130.
61. Suresh Chandra, *A Study in Ayer's Epistemology*, p. 168.
62. Ayer, *The Concept of a Person*, pp. 115-116.
63. *Ibid.*, p. 116.
64. Ayer, *The Concept of a Person*, p. 84.
65. Ayer, *The Concept of a Person*, p. 85.
66. Vide, *An Introduction of Logical Positivism*, p. 218.
67. J.P. Shukla, *The Nature of Mind*, p. 105.
68. R. Balasubramanian, The Pesonalistic Existentialism of Berdyaev, Centre of advance study in philosophy, University of Madras, pp. 26-27.

Bibliography

Ammerman, Robert R.: *Classics of Analytic Philosophy*, University of Wisconsin, Tata McGraw-Hill, Inc., New York, 1965.

Austin, J.L.: *Sense and Sensibilia*, Clarendon Press, Oxford, 1962.

Ayer, A.J.: *Language, Truth and Logic*, Gollancz, London, 1936.

Ayer, A.J.: *The Foundations of Empirical Knowledge*, Macmillan, London, 1940.

Ayer, A.J.: *Thinking and Meaning*, H.K. Lewis, London, 1947.

Ayer, A.J.: *Philosophical Essays*, Macmillan, London, 1954.

Ayer, A.J.: *The Revolution in Philosophy*, Macmillan, London, 1956.

Ayer, A.J.: *The Problem of Knowledge*, Penguin Books, 1956.

Ayer, A.J.: *Logic Positivism*, The Free Press of Glencoe, New York, 1959.

Ayer, A.J.: *The Concept of a Person*, Macmillan, London, 1963.

Ayer, A.J. : *The Origins of Pragmaticism*, Macmillan, London, 1968.

Ayer, A.J.: *Metaphysics and Common Sense*, Macmillan, London, 1969.

Ayer, A.J.: *Probability and Evidence*, Macmillan, London, 1972.

Ayer, A.J.: *The Central Questions of Philosophy*, Penguin Books, 1973.

Bahm, Archie, J.: *Philosophy - An Introduction*, University of New Mexico, Albuquerque, Asia Publishing House, 1953.

Barrett, W. and Henry D. Aiken, (eds.): *Philosophy in the Twentieth Century*, Vol. I, II, III, Random House, New York, 1962.

Berkeley, George, A.: *A Treatise Concerning the Principles of Human Knowledge*.

Bhattacharya, B.K.: *Logic, Value and Reality*, Calcutta University Press, 1961.

Bhattacharya, Kalidas: *Philosophy, Logic and Language*, Allied Publishers, Bombay, 1965.

Black, Max, (ed.): *Philosophical Analysis*, Prentice Hall, Inc., Englewood Cliffs, N.J., 1950.

Bradley, F.H.: *Appearance and Reality*, George Allen & Unwin, 1920.

Bradley, F.H.: *Ethical Studies*, Oxford, 1952.

Brightman, E.S.: *An Introduction to Philosophy*, Sir Issac Pitman & Sons Ltd., London, Revised Edition 1951.

Broad, C.D.: *Scientific Thought*, Kegan Paul, London, 1923.

Burnet, J.: *Greek Philosophy*, Macmillan, London, 1950.

Carnap, R.: *Philosophy and Logical Syntax*, Kegan Paul, London, 1935.

Chandra, Suresh: *A Study in Ayer's Epistemology*, Visva-Bharati, 1970.

Collingwood, R.G.: *An Essay on Philosophical Method*, The Clarendon Press, Oxford, 1950.

Copleston, F.: *Contemporary Philosophy*, Search Press, London, 1956.

Copy, Irving M.: *Introduction to Logic*, University of Hawai, Macmillan Publishing Co., Inc., New York, and Collier Macmillan Publishers, London, 1972.

Datta, D.M.: *The Chief Currents of Contemporary Philosophy*, The University of Calcutta, Calcutta University Press, 1961.

Dayakrishna: *The Nature of Philosophy*, Prachi Prakashan, Calcutta, 1956.

Descarates, Rene: *A Discourse of Method*, Trans. by John Veitch, J.M. Dant & Sons Ltd., London, 1960.

Durant, Will: *The Story of Philosophy*, Simon and Schuster, New York, 1952.

Edward, Paul and Pap, Arther, (eds.): *A Modern Introduction to Philosophy*, The Free Press, Glencoe, Illinois, 1957.

Ewing, A.C.: *The Fundamental Questions of Philosophy*, Allied Publishers, First Indian Edition, 1967.

Fakkenberg, R.: *History of Modern Philosophy*, Progressive Publishers, Calcutta, 1962.

Feigi, HJ. and Sellars, W., (eds.): *Readings in Philosophical Analysis*, Appleton - Century - Crofts, Inc., New York, 1949.

Fuller, B.A.G.: *A History of Philosophy*, Holt, Rinehart and Winston, Inc., New York, 1938.

Hampshire, S.: *Thought and Action*, Chatto and Windus, London, 1969.

Harries, E.E.: *Nature, Mind and Modern Science*, George Allen & Unwin, London, 1954.

Hospers, J.: *An Introduction to Philosophical Analysis*, Prentice-Hall, Inc., 1953.

Hume, David: *A Treatise of Human Nature* (L.A. Selby-Bigge), The Clarendon Press, Oxford, 1888.

Hume, David: *An Enquiry Concerning Human Understanding*, (L.A. Selby-Bigge), Oxford, 1902.

James, William: *Pragmatism*, Longmans, Green and Co., London, New Impression, 1910.

Joad, C.E.M.: *A Critique of Logical Positivism*, University of Chicago Press, 1950.

Kant, Immanual: *Critique of Pure Reason*, Trans. by N.K. Smith, The Macmillan and Co., Ltd. London, 1958.

Laird, John: *Problems of the Self*, Macmillan, London, 1917.

Locke, John: *An Essay Concerning Human Understanding*, Oxford, 1947.

Moore, G.E.: *Principia Ethica*, Cambridge University Press, London, 1903.

Moore, G.E.: *Philosophical Studies*, Routledge and Kegan Paul, London, 1922.

Moore, G.E.: *Some Main Problems of Philosophy*, Allen & Unwin, London, 1953.

Morris, C.W.: *Six Theories of Mind*, University of Chicago Press, 1932.

Muirhead, J.H.: *Contemporary British Philosophy* (ed.), Vol. I, Allen & Unwin, London, 1953.

Passmore, John: *A Hundred Year of Philosophy*, Penguin Books Inc., 1968, First Published by Duckworth, 1957.

Patrick, G.T.W.: *Introduction to Philosophy*. The Riberside Press, Cambridge.

Peter Freund, S.P. and Denise, T.C.: *Contemporary Philosophy and its Origins*, Affiliated East-West Press Pvt. Ltd., New Delhi, 1968.

Pitcher, George: *A Theory of Perception*, Princeton University Press, 1971.

Price, H.H.: *Perception*, Methuen, London, 1932.

Prince, H.H.: *Thinking and Experience*, Cambridge, Mass., Harvard University Press, 1953.

Rabel G.: *Kant*, Oxford University Press, 1963.

Radhakrishnan, S.: *History of Philosophy - Eastern and Western*, Vol. II, George Allen and Unwin, 1953.

Rai, Chhaya: *Kant Ka Niti Darshan*, Bhartiya Vidya Prakashan; Delhi, 1977.

Ramsay, F.P.: *The Foundations of Mathematics*, Kegan Paul, London, 1931.

Russell, B. and Whitehead, A.N.: *Principia Mathematics*, Cambridge, University Press, 1910.

Russell, B.: *The Problems of Philosophy*, Home University Library, London, 1912.

Russell, B.: *Our Knowledge of the External World*, Allen and Unwin, Londodn, 1914.

Russell, B.: *Introduction to Mathematical Philosophy*, Allen and Unwin, London, 1919.

Russell, B.: *An Inquiry into Meaning and Truth*, Allen & Unwin, London, 1940.

Russell, B.: *My Philosophical Development*, Allen and Unwin, London, 1959.

Rule, Gilbert: *The Concept of Mind*, Hutchinson & Co., 1958.

Schlick, N.: *Problems of Ethics*, Englewood Cliffs, N.J. : Prentice-Hall, 1939.

Schilpp, P.A., (ed.): *The Philosophy of Bertrand Russell*, Tudor Publishing Co., New York, Third Edition, 1951.

The Philosophy of G.E. Moore, Tudor Publishing Co., New York, Second Edition, 1952.

Shukla, J.P.: *The Nature of Mind*, Modern Book House, Jabalpur, 1966.

Stace, W.T.: *A Critical History of Greek Philosophy*, Macmillan, 1964.

Smullyan, Dietrichson, Keyt & Miller: *Introduction to Philosophy*, Prentice Hall of India Pvt. Ltd., New Delhi, 1967.

Taylor, A.E.: *Elements of Metaphysics*, Methuen, London, 1912.

Titus, Harold H. & Keeton, Morris T.: *The Range of Ethics*, Affiliated East-West Press Ltd., 1972.

Titus, Harold H.& Keeton, Morris T.: *The Range of Philosophy*, Affiliated East-West Press Pvt. Ltd., 1974.

Toulmin, S.: *Philosophy of Science*, Hutchinson, London, 1953.

Urmson, J.O.: *Philosophical Analysis*, Clarendon Press, Oxford, 1956.

Waismann, F.: *Introduction to Mathematical Thinking*, Hafner, London, 1951.

Warnock, G.J.: *English Philosophy Since 1900*, Oxford University Press, London, 1958.

Weber, Alferd: *History of Philosophy*, Charles Scribner's Sons, New York, 1925.

Weinberg, J.R.: *An Examination of Logical Positivism*, Kegan Paul, London; Harcourt, Brace & World, Inc., New York, 1936.

Whitehead, A.N.: *Science and The Modern World*, Cambridge University Press, 1946.

Whitehead, A.N.: *Adventures of Ideas*, Cambridge University Press, 1947.

Wittgenstein, L.: *Tractatus Logico - Philosophicus*, Trans. by D.F. Pears & B.F. McGuinness. The Humanities Press, New York, 1961.

Wittgenstein, L.: *Philosophical Investigations*, Blackwell, Oxford; Macmillan, New York, 1953.

Encyclopedia

The Encyclopedia of Philosophy, Vol. 1 to 8, Macmillan and Free Press, London.

Journals

Analysis 1933-34, Ayer, A.J., The Genesis of Metaphysics.

Analysis, 1934-35, Mace, C.A., Metaphysics and Emotive Language.

Analysis, 1934-35, Wisdom, J.O., The Analysis of Sense-Data.

Analysis, 1952-53, Armstrong, J.H., Knowledge and Belief.

Aristotelian Society, Supplementary Volume, 1937, Ayer, A.J., Does Philosophy Analyse Common Sense ?

Aristotelian Society, Supplementary Volumes, 1946, Austin, J.L., Other Minds.

Darshan International, Vol. VI, January 1966, Shrivastava, Jagdish Sahay, Basic Propositions.

Encounter, 108, September 1962, Popper, Karl R., On the Sources of Knowledge and of Ignorance.

Encounter 140, May 1965, Polanyi, Michael, On The Other Minds.

Indian Philosophical Quarterly, Vol. VI, No. 2, Jan. 1979, Shrivastava, V.S., Prof. Ayer's Conception of Sense-Data.

Journal of The Philosophical Association, July-Oct., 1958, Deshpande, D.Y.; Prasad, Rajendra; Mookerjee, S., A Priori and Empirical Propositions (I), (II), (III), respectively.

Mind, 1934, Ayer, A.J., Demonstration of the Impossibility of Metaphysics.

Philosophical Quarterly, 16, April, 1966, Hallie, Philip P., Wittgenstein's Exclusion of Metaphysical Nonsense.

Philosophical Review, 64, 1955, Penethum, Terence, Hume on Personal Identity.

Philosophical Review, 75, January, 1966, Shaffer, Jerome, Persons and Their Bodies.

Philosophy and Phenomenological Research, 4, June 1952, Werkmeister, W.H., Problems of Value Theory.

Philosophy and Phenomenological Research 27, Sept. 1966, Schlagel, Richard H., Science, Truth and Ordinary Language.

Philosophy and Phenomenological Research, 28, Dec. 1967, Johnstone, Henry Wl, Persons and Selves.

Philosophy and Phenomenological Research, 29, March, 1969, Daya Krishna, The Active and the Contemplative Values.

Review of Metaphysics, 18, Sept. 1964, Weiss, Paul, Our knowledge of What is Real.

Review of Metaphysics, 20, Sept. 1966, Ehman, Robutt R., Subjectivity and Solipsism.

Review of Metaphysics, 20, June 1967, Randall, John Herman, Metaphysics and Language.

The University Journal of Philosophy, April 1964, Chatterji, N.N., Are Value Propositions Meaningless?

Index